AN ASTROLOGY PRIMER
FOR THE MILLIONS

FOR THE MILLIONS SERIES

An Astrology Primer for the Millions
Borderline Oddities for the Millions
ESP for the Millions
ESP Development for the Millions
Famous Ghosts, Phantoms, and Poltergeists for the Millions
Handwriting Analysis for the Millions
Haunted Houses for the Millions
Hypnotism for the Millions
Mental Telepathy and ESP Powers for the Millions
Miracle Cures for the Millions
More ESP for the Millions
An Occult Dictionary for the Millions
Out-of-Body Experiences for the Millions
Phrenology for the Millions
Prophecy for the Millions
Psychic Self-Improvement for the Millions
Reincarnation for the Millions
Seances and Sensitives for the Millions
Spirit Communications for the Millions
A Supernatural Primer for the Millions
Tarot for the Millions
UFOs for the Millions
Understanding Dreams for the Millions
Yoga for the Millions

AN

ASTROLOGY

PRIMER

FOR THE

MILLIONS

by
Carl Payne Tobey

FOR THE MILLIONS SERIES

Sherbourne Press, Inc.   Los Angeles, California

Contents

CHAPTER I

Mystery of the Past

Astrology is older than any other branch of knowledge, and there is only speculation as to how it originated. But its mathematical base was too broad to have been a product of any primitive people. There may have been cave men and ancient primitives, because there are primitives today, just as there are advanced people. Our view of what the past has been is constantly changing. At the beginning of the century, people in our own country accepted the Biblical version of history and assumed the earth to be about 5000 years of age. Today, anthropologists and geologists talk of many millions of years. The Bible mentioned nothing about dinosaurs nor prehistoric elephants, but we have found their bones. At first, these monstrous beings were believed to have disappeared long before Man appeared, but then the bones of a prehistoric elephant with a spear in its body was discovered near the Mexican border in Arizona. It was difficult to believe that prehistoric elephants threw spears at one another, and it was guessed that man and prehistoric beings coexisted.

Beyond a few thousand years, we know little about the mysterious past. We have pieced a few bits of information together, allowing our imaginations to run wild, but always with the assumption that we of now are the greatest of all time. This is to be doubted.

Our greatest advance has been in the realm of mathematics. Without that, we could have no space program. And yet, our modern mathematics is but an extension and perfection of what the Greeks of 500 B.C. already knew. In recent years, due to the discovery of 50,000 clay tablets buried in the sand near the site of ancient Babylon, we now realize that most of what the Greeks knew in 500 B.C. was known to the Babylonians in 2000 B.C. The Babylonians may have known much more. The knowledge of the Babylonians may have come from some earlier civilization.

The average person is unaware that the Greeks had computed the circumference of the earth and the distance to the sun long before the birth of Christ. The concept of the earth being flat did not come until the Christians inaugurated it. Copernicus did not discover the sun as the center of the solar system. He merely advocated going back to the system of the ancient Greeks. Copernicus was an astrologer. The Greek mathematicians were astrologers. The mathematicians of all ancient cultures were astrologers. Before setting out to travel around the world, Columbus studied astrology.

Although the Catholic Church originally accepted and then ultimately outlawed astrology, the Bible remains filled with astrological symbolism. Neither science nor the church has been able to interpret these symbols, because they don't understand what astrology was. The first chapter of Genesis is a description of the zodiac, but it is incomplete. Part of it is missing, perhaps as the result of translators who did not understand what they were translating. The last chapter of the New Testament is filled with astrological symbols which are as yet uninterpreted. The ancient Arabs and Egyptians knew far more about astrology than we know today.

One of the greatest mysteries of astrology lies in the fact that its principles were known around the world, among peoples who knew nothing about each other. It was not confined to those countries that border the Mediterranean Sea. There was the astrology of the Chinese, of the Hindus, the Aztecs and the Mayans. Zodiacs were found by the first Spanish explorers in Mexico, Central and South America. They were somewhat different but not too different from the zodiac of the Mediterranean. The Aztec calendar was more perfect than the one we use today.

People see only what interests them. Since the Christian era began, most people have not seen astrology nor its symbols when it was in front of them because they were not interested in it. They were interested in something else. After digging it out of the ground, the Christians re-buried the Mexican calendar stone, because they feared it. It had to be re-discovered again. Most students of ancient cultures ignore the fact that all such cultures used astrology, merely because the students have no interest in astrology. It is not a part of the theories they have adopted. It might upset those theories. Dr. Ellsworth Huntington of Yale University, once noted as the world's most outstanding geographer, observed the similarity of zodiacs found around the world and he wondered about it. Did astrology develop independently in all of these separated cultures, or did it have a common origin? Bear in mind that these cultures were separated by great oceans, and these people are not supposed to have had much better transportation than rafts or canoes.

There are unsubstantiated traditions about the past. There are the traditions about Atlantis and Lemuria. Plato talked about Atlantis. It was a continent of high civilization and great culture in the south Atlantic. Tradition has it that this continent dropped into the sea destroying all of its population except that part of it which had previously migrated to Africa, perhaps to America, carrying some of its culture along. Traditions about Lemuria, sometimes called Mu, are similar, except that it was supposedly a continent in the South Pacific. In some great earthly upheaval, it is alleged to have sunk beneath the Pacific, but some of its inhabitants are supposed to have escaped to South America and possibly to the Orient. The religious custom of the Orient causes people to bow to the east, possibly to where the motherland disappeared. In South America, the ancient Indians bowed to the west. They would still be bowing in the direction of the supposed motherland. This is all tradition and speculation, and no proof exists, but it would be one explanation of why we find zodiacs in all parts of the world. We also find all kinds of structures around the world, built by unknown civilizations, to make astronomical measurements. Your guess about these things might prove as good as those of any other person. Present views are conditioned by the theories that people wish to uphold.

Knowledge coming from psychics is sometimes dependable and sometimes not, but it is odd that so many psychics around the world, while in trances, keep telling us about these lost continents.

All the zodiacs found around the world were divided

into twelve equal parts, which is a mathematical division. There is nothing in the heavens that is divided into twelve equal parts. Yet, this is a natural division found in many places in nature. The snowflake is always in the form of the hexagon, with six sides, but it is actually one design repeated twelve times, six times mirrored. This same design functions in the development of many minerals, although there are also other designs. These minerals, like snowflakes, develop independently, but always to the same design. There is the possibility that astrology developed independently and intuitively. Far removed persons often make the same mathematical and other discoveries. One discovery does not cause the other. There appears to be a central source of abstract and other knowledge that can be tapped. It would explain the strange talents of some of the psychics.

When we say that mathematics and astrology are abstract subjects, we mean they deal with the principles upon which the universe is built. They do not deal with causes as the term is usually applied. Both subjects are a study of design. People may have similarities but no two are exactly alike. To each life there is an abstract design. There is a design to your life that will apply to no other life. Astrology can tell you about it.

Astrology is like mathematics in another way. If you study arithmetic, which is one branch of mathematics, you can find it useful, even if you know nothing about geometry, logarithms or calculus. You can stop there or go on. You can study astrology from a minor or a major point of view. Whatever you might learn, it will be useful to you.

Greek mythology is a poetical distortion that grew out of astrology, but like the work of most poets, it won't actually teach you anything about astrology. It has no utility other than a study of its possible source. The ancients recognized various forces in nature and called them gods. We would call them dynamics, but they are still forces. Our American Indians also personalized human dynamics into gods.

Various cults must be credited with having preserved some of the knowledge of the ancients even if in distorted form. Through dark ages, people were not allowed to think for themselves. The church and the authorities insisted on telling them what they were allowed to think. Truths had to be taught in secret.

The Pythagorean schools of the Greeks were secret schools. Students were sworn not to reveal the knowledge they gained. It was the cults and the secret schools that succeeded in preserving some knowledge of astrology even if bady distorted. The Rosicrucians and the Theosophists were among the secret schools, although it is difficult to know whether modern Rosicrucians have any connection with the old orders. The principal astrological book store in the U.S. is also a Masonic supply company. We do not know whether the Masons actually preserved any astrological knowledge. According to Manly Hall, the biggest astrological library in the world is at the Vatican, but the Catholic Church does not teach any astrology to its members. In the New York Public Library, astrological books are kept under lock and key, where the public cannot reach them, even if they are actually the property of the public. The masses are still too young to be told the truth. Suppression of astrology was instrumented by the churches which were anxious to keep the people under their control. Academicians have given close to 100 percent cooperation. Astronomy came into being after 500 A.D. in an effort to conform with the dictates of the church. Astronomy was to be nothing more than a materialistic science. Most remarkable of all is the fact that astrology survived at all. The cults which kept some semblance of astrology alive had to be made up of brave and daring people. A slip of the tongue often meant the loss of one's head or a burning at the stake. If the information of the cults was faulty, it was better than no information at all. It was better than following the dogma of the blind leaders of the churches. Therefore, we owe a debt to the cults and secret orders.

Religions are in conflict with each other. It is one dogma opposing another dogma. Science is supposed to be different, but it is not too different, at least not at the academic level. The Space Age may be changing that. Schools and universities teach children a certain amount of truth while brainwashing them into modern superstitions. One of these superstitions is the claim that astrology is an ancient superstition.

In India and other parts of the Orient, astrology is accepted by almost everyone, even if it is a crude astrology. Hindu doctors connected with American institutions and Hindu students in the United States often ask the writer, "Why is the United States so prejudiced against astrology." These are people educated in America. Meanwhile, the whole subject of modern medicine grew out of astrology. Hypocrates, known as the father of medicine, was an astrologer. Paracelsus, known as the father of modern medicine, was an astrologer. Yet, long before either of these men, the Egyptians had physicians and surgeons, while the oldest tribes had their medicine men. Savages knew much about the value of herbs as medicine. It was passed down to them from somewhere.

We can go back 3000 years into history and have at least a distorted and very incomplete version of what was going on. Beyond that, everything becomes foggy and vague. If men were living in caves at a given time, that does not mean that other men were not living in mansions at the same time. The academic view likes to visualize civilization as on the rise, but it may have been on a long decline before it began to rise again. There may have been cultures greater than ours. A person familiar with the vast and complicated realms of mathematical knowledge of the ancient astrology is likely to realize that this is the work of a culture superior to ours in many respects. The true origin of astrology is hidden. It is something that we know nothing about. It is a greater mystery than the origin of mathematical thinking. Back beyond the Babylonians of 2000 B.C., everything becomes foggy and vague. We can speculate and guess, but we don't know. Astrology may have come from Atlantis and Lemuria, but we don't know whether there was an Atlantis or Lemuria.

CHAPTER II

Astrology in the Twentieth Century

As we turned from the eighteenth to the ninteenth century, Sir Isaac Newton was studying and writing about astrology, and although his writings still exist, their publication has never been allowed. To see them, you must have sufficient influence to gain permission. Although the New York Public Library has books on astrology, you must have enough influence to get permission to see them. No university in the United States will teach you anything about astrology. The materialists have fought like tigers to suppress astrology. This campaign has been engineered principally from the astronomical department of Harvard University.

Until the crash in the stock market of 1929, few people knew the difference between the words astronomy and astrology. There are claims that the founding fathers of the country employed astrology in its making. Benjamin Franklin certainly had an interest in the subject. He gave astrological advice in *Poor Benjamin's Almanack* (sic.) which supposedly evolved into the *Saturday Evening Post*. Aside from the *World Almanac*, all almanacs had an astrological base. It was their original purpose.

Theodore Roosevelt kept his horoscope engraved on metal near his white house desk, and was said to consult it frequently. The interest in astrology of Franklin D. Roosevelt was never clear, but he always wrote and thanked any astrologer who sent his astrological views. His wife, Eleanor, was more vocal. She admitted her interest, in a magazine article, but questioned the accuracy of the art of prediction. She praised astrology's usefulness in determining human characteristics. In 1908, an astrologer named John Hazelrigg predicted that the men elected President of the U.S. in 1920, 1940 and 1960 would all die in office. They did. In early months of 1929, the *New York Post* carried the prediction of an Hoboken astrologer who said the stock market would fall apart and crash in October of that year. It did.

In the early part of the century, a colorful woman appeared in New York. She had moved down from Boston. Her name was Evangeline Adams. She had an office in Carnegie Hall, and it cost $25.00 an hour to see her. She became a mystery to talk about. Broadway talked about her, and Wall Street talked about her. You practically had to know somebody to get an appointment with her. She was an astrologer, J. P. Morgan was one of her clients. Enrico Caruso was another. Actors and actresses flocked to see her. As she was getting old and a bit feeble, radio came into its own, and a toothpaste company put her on the air. At 6:00 P.M. every night, millions tuned in to Evangeline Adams and listened to her talk about astrology. She wrote several best-selling books, the one gaining most attention being *The Bowl of Heaven* in which she told the story of her life.

Evangeline Adams made a prediction about the first Lindbergh baby over the air. It was said that Lindbergh didn't like it and complained. Rumor had it that this complaint forced the astrologer off the air. This writer interviewed an official of the broadcasting company about it. He denied the story, but finally admitted there was a complaint, as he read the file himself. He said, "We didn't put her off the air. We just didn't renew her contract."

In *Science* magazine, Bart J. Bok, a Harvard astronomer bragged that he and his colleagues used sufficient influence to get the Federal Communications Commission to bar astrology from the air. A ruling said that you could not present astrology unless as fiction or unless you were against it. To please the powers, when the broadcasters drew up their own code, they copied this ruling, and up till this writing, it is still in their code. Many radio and television stations now ignore it.

1932 was an important year for astrology. Two astrology magazines appeared on newsstands. The first, *Destiny*, lasted only a few months. The second, *American Astrology*, became very successful and is still on newsstands. It was edited by Paul G. Clancy, who was out to make America astrology conscious. The publication is edited today by Joanne Clancy. *Wynn's Astrology Magazine* soon appeared, edited by Sydney K. Bennett, who also wrote an astrology newspaper column for the *Chicago Tribune-N.Y. Daily News* syndicate. The publication continued until Bennett tired of editing it, stopped publication and went to New Zealand to live. Soon after *American Astrology's* success was known, *Horoscope* appeared on newsstands. These two magazines have always led the field. The first editor of *Horoscope* was Marion Meyer Drew, but Grant Lewi soon took her place. He had previously taught English at Dartmouth. He edited *Horoscope* for many years. His books became very popular. He was finally followed by Edward A. Wagner, who edits the magazine today. Wagner was a former Ohio newspaper man, but he had previously edited a student astrology publication and had written an astrological newspaper column for the Hearst papers. Leaving *Horoscope*, Marion Meyer Drew became editor of a new publication called *Astrology Guide*. She was followed by Dal Lee, whose interest in astrology is of a more religious nature. He, sort-of, sees astrology as the language of God. He is an interesting authority of the history of astrology in religion. There have been many other astrology magazines. Some fell by the wayside. Some were not run by astrologers, merely by publishers.

The astrology magazines have been the principle instrument in building today's modern interest in astrology. It is safe to say that a million people in the United States buy some kind of an astrology publication every month. The newspaper column has the greatest following, and the column of Sydney Omarr leads this field. It is published in more than 300 American newspapers, but is also syndicated in many languages around the world.

In nearly all big cities there is some bookstore that specializes in astrological books. There are many such books, not so many good ones.

The average person of today knows the sign "under which he was born." There are few women who are not conscious of astrology. They seem to have an intuitive conception of an overall design to life, and they find it in astrology. They soon sell their husbands on the idea.

About two-thirds of the following of astrology is among women.

The *envelope product* is another source of astrology interest. This is another newsstand product sold from a rack. There are twelve envelopes, one for each month of birth or zodiacal sign. There is the *Voice of Astrology*, originally written by Alma Granning and now by Gwen Stiefold. Then, there is *Ushers*, put out by Frances Usher of the old vaudeville team.

There are many other publications. We must not overlook the fact that, like many other subjects, including all religion and most any subject you might want to name, astrology has its crackpot and neurotic following. This is nothing against astrology. Until the space age, most of the people teaching astronomy were crackpots, filled with dogma and prejudice and knowing very little of anything about their subject of astronomy. Most of the people following or studying psychology had a mental problem or they would never have become interested in psychology in the first place. If you want to learn astronomy, study the subject and not astronomers. If you want to study astrology, study the subject itself, not its followers.

Let's face it, an astrological chart of birth can tell you more about an individual than all the psychiatrists and doctors in the country can find out in a life-time, and yet, the sum total of what we know about astrology today is but the finite, while the unknown possibilities are infinite. Astrologers are somewhat inclined to go beyond what they can actually do. Most of them are too inclined to accept theories such as karma and reincarnation without proof, merely because it seems reasonable. Reasonable means only that which appears to fit in with your prejudice or what you already know, and our total knowledge is still infinitesimal when related to the whole.

It is doubtful whether we could find any astrological publication anywhere that did not warn John F. Kennedy about his danger of assassination. The astrologers were all predicting the death of Franklin D. Roosevelt before it happened. Yet none even hinted the death of Coolidge, Hoover, Truman or Eisenhower. For the month of April, 1945, Alma Granning led off her forecast with, "The flag at the Whitehouse will be at half-mast this month."

RCA Communications Inc. employs the planets to predict magnetic storms. These predictions go to every U.S. Air Force base in the world. The information is vital in handling communications.

Many of the largest corporations in the country buy weather services that are based on planetary motion. George McCormack has long been noted for his astrological weather predictions. A meteorologist in Colorado Springs uses the planets to predict weather, but he does not call it astrology. Edward A. Wagner, editor of *Horoscope* is also a meteorologist. Dr. Andrew Ellicott Douglass, noted astronomer of the University of Arizona and one-time president of that university, also creator of dendochronology, the tree ring science, as well as the discover of cosmic light, wrote a book before he died, claiming that planets cause weather. The book was suppressed. There is some promise that it may be published in the not-too-distant future by the University of Arizona Press.

The professors will say, "This is not astrology." Stop kidding anybody. When you use the planets to predict the future, what is it? Even the cloistered *Science* magazine published the work of Donald A. Bradley illustrating that there is an apparent connection between moon phases and rain.

The part that astrology plays in business today is a closely guarded secret. J. P. Morgan employed astrology. This writer could name many giants of industry who today use astrology, but this would be a violation of confidence. The business man looks at things differently than the professor. Things have to work for him. He would prefer that others do not know his trade secrets. His purpose is not to reform or cure the world. It is to make money.

Edward R. Dewey heads the Foundation for the Study of Cycles, at the University of Pittsburgh. There are cycles everywhere. Mr. Dewey investigates cycles. All sciences are filled with cycles of some kind. Mr. Dewey's job is to find out what causes them. The FSC publishes monthly bulletins relating to this work. You can obtain them by becoming a member of the Foundation for the Study of Cycles. The work has been largely financed by the Chicago multi-millionaire, W. Clement Stone.

The fact that most of the men who made great astronomical discoveries prior to the twentieth century were actually astrologers was well-covered by Joseph Goodavage in *Analog* magazine, which also ran tests to illustrate how well the weather can be predicted by astrology.

Despite the fact that astronomers are open enemies of astrology on the surface, this writer has acted as an astrological advisor to a number of the most prominent astronomers in their personal lives. The writer also knows space scientists who are employing astrology. One of my students is now a designer of advanced electronic computers. This writer has taught astrology to almost every kind of engineer.

The most exciting book on astrology that has come out in modern times is *My World of Astrology* by Sydney Omarr. It has far outsold any astrological book that has been published during the last thirty years. It was published by Fleet Publishing Company. It tells the story of the unfortunate career of Dr. Roy K. Marshall, former head of Fels Planetarium in Philadelphia, who set out to destroy astrology, and wound up in a mental institution.

There have not been very many good books published on astrology during this century.

Astrology has had its impact on psychology in recent years. Dr. Marc Edmund Jones, who holds a Ph.D. in psychology granted by Columbia University, is an astrologer. Vernon Clark, psychologist of Evanston, Ill., employs astrology in his work. One of the greatest in the field of psychiatry, Dr. Carl Jung, was an astrologer. Many psychologists have tried to deny this, but let us quote briefly from Jung's own statements. These are some of Dr. Jung's remarks when interviewed by *Astrologie Moderne.*

"There have been many striking analogies between the astrological and the psychological event or the horoscope and the characterological disposition . . . One can expect with considerable assurance that a given well-defined psychological situation will be accompanied by an analogous astrological configuration. Astrology consists of configurations symbolic of the collective unconscious, which is the subject matter of psychology."

In another interview, Dr. Jung stated that he never

treated a patient without first consulting the patient's horoscope.

A national group of physicians, psychologists, psychiatrists and chiropractors have been at work investigating astrology and disease for over three years. Their findings are likely to be published at some time in the future. The greatest factor that has prevented astrology from expanding and developing in the direction that it should be going is lack of research funds. People have strange attitudes. The man who will give away a million dollars for research in other fields takes everything he can out of astrology, but never puts anything back in. Perhaps the time is not right. Charles Fort put it this way, "You steamboat when comes steamboat time." Astrologers are ahead of their time insofar as this era is concerned, but the time will come.

The American Federation of Astrologers has its headquarters at 6 Liberty Court, S.E., Washington, D.C. Communities and some states have laws against practicing astrology. Some states recognize astrology. You can obtain a license to practice astrology in Ohio if you can pass their examination. It would be against the law to lend a book on astrology to a friend in Phoenix, but the law has never been enforced. Phoenix bookstores sell astrology books, and Phoenix newsstands display all of the astrology magazines. Walk into a cocktail party in any millionaire's home, and you will find that most everybody there can tell you "under what sign he was born." There are two kinds of college professor, the one who turns up his nose at astrology and the one who studies it in secret. Our universities have a long way to go before they will tolerate free-thinking professors. To a certain extent, universities in the United States and England are still brainwashing institutions. The college professor can keep his mouth shut and keep his job.

The *Wall Street Journal* of Dow Jones has treated news of the world of astrology very impartially. It has run accounts of conventions of the American Federation of Astrologers on page one. It quoted one broker as saying that clients using astrology do better than other clients. It has particularly noted the work of LCDR David Williams, president of the Astrologer's Guild in New York. In June 1965, it credited him with having accurately predicted the last two recessions in the stock market.

CHAPTER III

What Is the Zodiac?

The zodiac divides the space around the earth into twelve equal parts. To one living on the earth, the sun appears to go through these twelve divisions with the seasons. By knowing your date of birth, it is possible to know the sign the sun was in when you were born. The moon and planets also go through the same zodiac but in different periods. The moon gets around in 28 days, Mars in two years, Jupiter in 12 years, Saturn in 29 years, Uranus in 84 years, Neptune in 165 years, etc. The trip of each body around the zodiac represents a cycle. This can become very complicated, but we will treat its more simple phases here. This is only an introduction, but what you learn here you can use.

The zodiac has nothing to do with the fixed stars, although the poets have linked it to them. The zodiac is the equivalent of a mathematical formula; but there is no formula so interesting. The zodiac catalogues people and illustrates the principles that motivate them. You can learn much about yourself and about other people from the zodiac. This book will give you a start. If you become enthusiastic, you can keep going further and further. There is no limit to what you can learn. You can get to recognize the characteristics of the mob or crowd and understand why it does whatever it happens to do at a given time. Astrology will give you a new conception of time. Time has to be something different from what we think it is.

Think of a sheet of paper going in all directions to infinity. We would call that a plane in space. Or think of the top of a flat desk. Anything at the same level as the top of the desk, at any distance, is said to be the same plane as the top of the desk.

The zodiac is in the plane of the earth's orbit around the sun, which is called the ecliptic. Now, we take the point in that plane where it crosses the plane of the equator. We use that point as a starting point for our measurements. This point does not stay fixed in its relation to the fixed stars. It moves with them.

Using the center of the earth as our center, we draw lines out to the mathematical point described above. You won't have to do this. We are just explaining it. Once we have the circle of space around the earth divided into twelve equal parts in the plane of the earth's orbit, we identify these twelve spaces as the twelve *signs of the zodiac*. Everything in nature works and functions in accord with the principles of the zodiac. Each *sign* represents an important principle of nature.

In your life or any other life, there are two purposes; a conscious and an unconscious purpose. The conscious purpose is *your* purpose. The one of which you are unconscious is nature's purpose. You will have much more control over your life if you know what nature's purpose is. In other words, what is nature trying to do with your life? Let's take a very concrete illustration. Consider the act of sex. When two people have sex relations, their purpose is personal pleasure, but nature's purpose is procreation, the production of children, and the perpetuation of the race or species.

Take another example. You eat to satisfy your hunger, but nature has her purpose. She creates your hunger in order to replenish your body and keep it alive and functioning.

Nature has her own purpose always, but she is very secretive about it. When we study the twelve principles of the zodiac, we learn more and more about what nature is trying to do. She is constantly balancing life and then throwing it off balance, perhaps to keep you awake and conscious, but she also causes you to grow tired and sleep to give her time to completely have control while she works on your body to keep it healthy, but she allows you to dream, and often supplies messages in your dreams if you can interpret them. All the principles involved with these functions of nature are mathematically represented in the twelve signs of the zodiac.

The same principles represented by the signs of the zodiac are also represented by the planets, sun and moon, and in a surprising way. In the same manner and order that the principles go around the zodiac, they accord with the mean distance of the planets from the earth.

Of the twelve basic principles involved, they come in pairs. Two signs will represent opposite phases of the same principle. When we come to a discussion of the signs of the zodiac, we will discuss them in pairs, for they will be easier to understand when we do.

We will sometimes use the word rule, as when we say that Mars rules Scorpio. We do not use the word *rule* meaning to rule like a king. We employ it to mean measure. We are always measuring in astrology.

Each planet and sign of the zodiac is important in your horoscope, but some factors are more important than others.

To know your whole horoscope, it would be necessay to know your exact moment of birth. Yet, we can go a long way even when we don't know it. A man who has lived his entire life in Chicago can know most everything to know about Chicago, but he may know little about San Francisco. The degree of the zodiac coming over that point where the earth's orbital plane crosses the eastern horizon at the moment of your birth is one of the most important factors of the horoscope, but we can't know that unless your time of birth is accurately known. This mathematical point is called the Ascendent. The four most important factors in a horoscope are the Ascendent, the Sun, the Moon and the Secondary Ascendent, which we won't have time to talk about here.

All children born on a certain day, month and year will have a similar pattern to their lives, but many things will be different also. Every few minutes changes something, and the place of birth will make a difference. Heredity will make a very great difference. The best way to realize the effect of heredity will be to consider it in its broadest scope. An elephant might be born on the same day as a great pianist, but the elephant will never make a great pianist because of his heredity. The pianist was born with fingers. That had nothing to do with his horoscope. It involved his heredity. His ancestors had fingers. The ancestors of the elephant did not.

All the people born from March 21st through April 19th will have the Sun in Aries. To a certain extent, regardless even of their year of birth, these people will have characteristics in common that other people do not have. In other respects, they will be quite different.

There is a good deal of confusion in the public mind about the dates when the Sun changes from one sign to another. That is due to the imperfection of our calendar. Our year is not exactly 365 days nor quite exactly 365.25 days. We partially correct the error by adding a day to leap year, and then eliminating one leap year out of every hundred years. But, that isn't strictly accurate either. Again, the Sun might change from Aries to Taurus at 3:14 P.M. in the afternoon, in which event people born before 3:14 P.M. would have the Sun in Aries, but people born after 3:14 P.M. would have the Sun in Taurus. You can see how much work the professional astrologer must do when he works everything out to the minute for you.

If you were born on the day, mentioned above, you could probably decide for yourself which of two signs might be correct for you, but you might be born in the morning when the Sun was in Aries but when the sign Taurus was on the Ascendent, and then you would have the characteristics of both signs. In this book, we are going to tell you only about the sun signs, but some information we will give you has never been published in a book before.

Now, let us list the twelve signs and pair them off as we find them in astrology.

SIGN	*RULED BY*
Cancer	Moon
Gemini	"Z" undiscovered
Taurus	"Y" undiscovered
Aries	Pluto
Pisces	Neptune
Aquarius	Uranus
Leo	Sun
Virgo	Mercury
Libra	Venus
Scorpio	Mars
Sagittarius	Jupiter
Capricorn	Saturn

The birthdays when the Sun will be in these various signs of the zodiac will be as follows:

Cancer (June 22nd to July 22nd)
Gemini (May 20th to June 21st)
Taurus (April 20th to May 19th)
Aries (March 21st to April 19th)
Pisces (February 19th to March 20th)
Aquarius (January 20th to February 18th)
Leo (July 23rd to August 22nd)
Virgo (August 23rd to September 22nd)
Libra (September 23rd to October 22nd)
Scorpio (October 23rd to November 21st)
Sagittarius (November 22nd to December 21st)
Capricorn (December 22nd to January 19th)

To be a true type of any sign, a person would have to be born at sunrise when all the planets were in the same sign as the Sun. This has never happened, insofar as we know, although we have come close. Thus, we won't find many people who are pure types, although we find some who are very one-sided.

Get yourself a note-book if you want to learn this subject. Collect the birth dates of all the people you know, your friends, relatives, etc. Segregate them. Place all the Aries people on one page, all the Taurus people on another page, with their birth data. When you have the birthdays segregated, study all the people of one sign in connection with what we have to say about these people here. Study the opposite characteristics in the sign that pairs off the first sign and the people you have listed for that sign. In this way, you will begin to become conscious of the principles involved. There will be exceptions to the rule because of other astrological factors you have not studied yet, but you will be surprised at how well the majority of people will fit into the picture.

Let us give you a word of advice. After you read this book, read it again. It has been our experience that the student who reads a text again and again, perhaps five times, is the one who picks up and grasps the concepts. Students taking the writer's correspondence course in astrology often write in, "Each time I read a lesson, I see more that was there all the time, but I didn't see it on previous readings." You must constantly compare what you read here with your own experience. This will be a life-long process, because you will never stop noting new facts that you had not observed before. This book is only your first grade. You will actually learn the most from your own experience in life. You will begin to see and recognize what has been around you all of the time, but you were not expecting it, so you did not see it. People are inclined to unconsciously ignore what is around them unless it conforms to what they already know. This is another principle that is always at work. Society at large ignores what does not fit in with its preconceived conclusions. That is why educators have found it so easy to ignore astrology, but they are finding it more difficult to do every day. There are many realms of knowledge that society ignores, but you can make this your asset. You can be the individual who learns not to ignore what you see. A trained air pilot will recognize a type of a plane at a great distance. The layman does not see what the pilot sees. The pilot knows what he is looking for. You will soon get to know much about people that others do not see, merely because you are looking and other people are not.

CHAPTER IV

Cancer and Leo

*(Cancer Born June 22nd through July 22nd.
Leo Born July 23rd through August 22nd.)*

An extrovert is an outgoing person, one who freely expresses his personality, while an introvert is a person inclined to live within himself. These two terms beautifully express the zodiacal signs Cancer and Leo. Cancer is the introvert, Leo the extrovert.

Cancer is always somewhat the baby whose feelings are so easily hurt. The Cancer woman expects the parents and all men to treat her like a baby and take care of her. She isn't a baby when it comes to being able to take care of herself. She capitalizes on her ability to make other people take care of her. Meanwhile, she will be secretly hiding her money and setting it aside for a rainy day. If her husband goes broke and is down and out, he will suddenly get a surprise. She will come to the rescue. Meanwhile, she can be very lovable, but she usually has any situation under her personal control. She reads and understands men like a book. While they are feeling sorry for her, she is mothering them. She is pretty likely to come out on top, but she will never be secure because she is basically insecure. At the very base of her nature is the fear of starvation. No matter how much money she may ever have, that fear is there, and almost constantly, there is that constant awareness of the possibility. She wants money hidden away somewhere, so she will know where to go to get it when the fatal day comes. If she has been described as domestic, she isn't really, because she detests housework. Yet, she likes kitchens, because that is where food is usually kept. Although she may not be conscious of it, the people she likes are people who take her to dinner, or invite her to dinner. They spell security to her. She may not necessarily be a big eater, but she is happier and more content when she knows there is lots of food around. She likes to go to the best eating places, and the most expensive so long as somebody else is paying the bill. She will probably do very well in business because she is always practical about the economic end of things. For a husband, she will select a man who she believes is going to make money for her, and she will want to manage the money, which she can do very well. She may love her children, but she won't want her husband to love them more than he loves her. Not all, but a good ratio of Cancer women will have well developed breasts. After all, they are symbolic of food. The ancients symbolized Cancer with the crab, which has a shell and is tenacious. These people are tenacious, and they can easily crawl into their shells. They can be *hurt* when they don't get what they want, but that is one of the ways they get it.

Before switching to a consideration of Cancer men, let us make a point clear. No sign is better or worse than another sign. No sign is evil while another is good. They all have their purposes. They all have a good place in life, but with every sign those purposes can be misused and misapplied. Thus, if this writer appears to be critical or enthusiastic about any sign, that is his error. Life could not exist if any one of these basic principles were to be excluded. All signs and all the principles they represent are necessary to the existence of society. In some way, we all need each other. In some way, we are all necessary to the whole. If Cancer appears to be selfish, that is why it is able to come to, and does come to, the rescue at the last moment. It may wait till the last moment to see if someone else won't do the rescuing, but it won't be too late. So, let's consider Cancer men.

Statistics will prove that Cancer men are more successful financially than any other group. In the volume

Who's Who in Commerce and Industry, summer birth dates predominate and rate above all others, but of summer birthdates, Cancer is definitely at the top. On the other hand, in the volume *Who's Who in America*, which is heavily weighted by academicians and professional birthdays, winter birth dates predominate. Summer birth dates are at a minimum.

As a youth, the Cancer man is anxious to get out making money. That lure of making money may take him away from his education. While he is still in school, he may be working on the side, making money and setting it aside. Even if he happens to come from a wealthy family, he will want to prove to himself that he can make money himself. The Cancer man also acts the part of the baby, and succeeds in having other people *take care* of him. He will be surrounded by people who feel it is necessary for them to look after him. They don't seem to believe him capable of looking after himself, but he is. His favorite expression is, "I'm just a poor boy trying to get along." He will continue to use it after he has a few million dollars hidden away. Everybody around him feels sorry about him, and they worry about him. He knows that, and that's what he wants. John D. Rockefeller Sr. was Cancer. So is his grandson, Nelson Rockefeller. If these Cancer people may appear greedy, make no mistake about one thing; they are sympathetic and charitable. They will give to the needy, but they have no intention of giving where it is not needed. They do not intend to be suckers. They are very careful about what they do with money. In the main, they live their lives within themselves, and they are introverts, but they are not lone wolves. They need company. You won't find them alone. They always surround themselves with people. They can be afraid if left completely alone. They would not be comfortable in solitude. There would be something fearful about life. They understand people. They can play on people the way a pianist plays on a piano. They often do well in politics, but in a very quiet way. They do the trading. They find out what other people need, and they supply those needs at a profit to themselves. Study the political technique of Nelson Rockefeller. His slogan was, "He cared." He campaigned in grocery stores where he was close to food. Meanwhile, he made money building grocery stores and supermarkets in Venezuela. Another successful Cancer politician was Calvin Coolidge.

Now, let us consider the exact opposite of Cancer, the sign Leo. Self-interest is vital to both signs, and yet they are opposites. Cancer is the introvert, Leo the extrovert. Cancer trades. Leo leads. Cancer is retiring. Leo is full of self that has to be expressed. Leo is the big brother. He does not have the Cancer shrewdness. What he wants, he demands, and expects his demands to be met. Yet, he is kind. His greatest enjoyment is doing things for people. He enjoys being the man to whom the weak go for assistance—for strength. He has strength. Here is pride at its utmost. Cancer can bury pride, but not Leo. He doesn't want favors from other people. It hurts his pride to accept favors from others. He is no baby, while Cancer is content to play the role of the baby. Leo could never be the poor boy trying to get along. He wouldn't ever want anybody to think of him as poor. He thinks of himself as big and strong, and he wants others to think of him that way. The material things of life are secondary. He has spirit. It is his spirit that counts. His image of himself is vitality and he is vitality.

If Cancer appears shy or timid, Leo is self-confidence itself. Think of Napoleon and de Gaulle, both Leos. Leo can be the showman. Here is both royalty and loyalty combined. Leo can give away what it might need itself, on the theme that someone else needs it more. Under some circumstances, there might be some arrogance, but there is always some negative side of any sign that can show up. On the other hand, there can be a certain magnificence about this sign. It is the showman on parade. Houdini and Ethel Barrymore were both Leos. These people may be found showing other people how to solve their problems as if there was nothing to it. Leo is said to be ruled by the Sun, and symbolically to have the strength of the Sun. It is a sign that can be very

cheerful, good natured and optimistic. It may be posses-
sive, but it takes care of those it possesses. Its motivation
comes from within, and it is not easily swayed nor influ-
enced.

What about the Leo women? They are likely to be
quite self-sufficient. Husbands are usually dependent on
them in many ways. Yet, we don't very often find the
Leo wife taking the stage away from her husband. She
wants to build him up, and if he can handle himself, she
will sit back and watch him with pride. She is a partner
rather than a dependent. She will probably know the
neighbors and might run the neighborhood. People can
depend on her if she is needed. She likes people and likes
to mix with them. Unlike Cancer, you won't find her
retiring into any shell. She can glow. The ancient symbol of this sign was the lion. If you don't give these
people attention, while they won't crawl into their
shells, they may disappear. They will go where people
will give them attention. If the husband of a Leo girl
fails to give his wife attention, she'll be getting it elsewhere. There will be plenty of people who will want to
give her attention. She doesn't fear strangers because she
likes people, and she can take care of herself. She isn't
likely to fear the unknown because God is on her side,
or she feels that He is. She has all the inner security that
the Cancer woman lacks. She enjoys action, going
places, meeting new people, seeing new scenery. She is

alive. Like the Leo man, she has to be expressing herself. She will find a way of doing it somewhere. She worries less about the uncertainties of life, and lives more in the future than in the past. She isn't too concerned with conventions. She makes the rules as she goes along. If she has children, she is a good mother, and the children never seem to be a problem to her. She can take things in her stride. She likes to laugh and be gay. She enjoys most forms of entertainment and perhaps sports. She is capable of showing much affection. Even if modest, she is strong within herself. She isn't the gold-digger type, which Cancer can be. She likes to have everything nice, but other things are much more valuable to her than gold. Nevertheless, she is likely to have a heart of gold. All Leo people probably like to be the bearers of good news. They just like to cheer up other people. For this reason, they are nice to have around. In astrology, we have a Leo. He is Sydney Omarr. Most of the celebrities are his friends. They are always running to him for helpful advice. He doesn't charge them for it. He seems to enjoy being the big brother. Leo can organize people, get them working together, and tell them what to do. They can solve differences by putting everybody in a better mood and making them all feel better and happier within themselves.

CHAPTER V

Gemini and Virgo

(Gemini Born May 20th through June 20th.
Virgo Born August 23rd through September 22nd.)

These two signs are closely related to the nervous system. They are signs of communication, but the mind of Virgo is built to deal with material things, while the mind of Gemini deals with ideas, principles and abstractions. They can both be restless, but Gemini is a very restless sign. It is difficult for these people to sit still. They have to be moving around. Virgo is a disciplined sign. The Virgo lives in accord with the rules, even when not understanding what they are all about. Gemini is more likely to change the rules for each occasion, or for each day. Gemini wants to know why, while Virgo is more often satisfied with the authorities, more inclined to go along with the authorities.

Tradition has always held that the weak spot of Gemini is the lungs, of Virgo the bowels. It is probable that both of these factors have something to do with the nervous system. Gemini may never be too content because of that restlessness. The mind gets around and thinks of many things. You find many writers born under Gemini, but they are usually writers of short material. They don't like to stay with any one subject too long. For this reason, they are never monotonous. You usually find quite a number of these people around a newspaper office. They are not dogmatists. They can argue one side of a subject one day, the other side the next day. If they are ever contented, it is when they are moving from place to place. They need much in the way of new scenery. Seldom do they become anybody's enemies because no one interests them that long, and they can usually have a pretty fair understanding of how the other fellow feels about things. One of their great weaknesses is that they can't make up their minds, or having made up their minds they change them. The sign is said to represent the double personality. The symbol was the twins, and it is interesting to note that all zodiacs found around the world always portrayed this sign with two people. In Europe, it was twin children, while in one American zodiac, it was two soldiers. Statistics of the U.S. Census Bureau disclose that more multiple births take place at this time of year than at any other season. Figures from England are the same. Yet, long before there was a Bureau of the Census, the ancients around the world knew all about this and left the story in their symbols. *Scientists* were never able to read them.

In romance and love, this sign thinks again in terms of principles. A mate is an idea. Many people might satisfactorily conform to the idea. Two Ford cars of the same model are about identical. The Gemini woman can accept a new mate if he is the same make and model. The Gemini men are not different in this respect. Its not the individual person that counts. It is the abstract design to which the individual is built. Other people may not understand this, with the result that they may consider these people frivolous. They are loyal to principles and designs rather than to people or material things. Yet, they like people, because they find people interesting. Probing into what makes people tick helps sooth the Gemini curiosity. There can be a bit of the hobo in Gemini. Travel can be good for the Gemini soul. The Gemini mind thinks fast, and it can go around in many circles. There can be a good sense of humor. John F. Kennedy was the only Gemini President the United States ever had. Jim Farley was another Gemini. A typical one was the former Mayor James Walker of New York. Secretary McNamara of Defense is a Gemini, but he hasn't proved to be the warrior type. The great problem of these people is deciding which side they are on. They can't make up their minds. Remember J. F. Kennedy trying to make up his mind what to do about the Bay of Pigs. We can always remember Marilyn Monroe as a Gemini woman. Although we can't think of Gemini as too much of a worrying sign, it is always arguing with itself.

As a sign, Virgo can do the worrying, but Virgo lives on a material rather than on an abstract plane. These people are apt to believe you are what you eat. They are very conscious of what enters the mouth. The sign likes vitamins. There may be health foods around. There are a good many prudes born under the sign. These people are also very conscious of their dress. They like to be on the dignified side, but they like to dress "right." They know the rules of etiquette and abide by them. They can be hard workers, and they will keep the work well-organized. They are good observers of all the details, how a word is spelled, where the knife and fork should be, what so-and-so wore at the party, the date and time of day when Joe and Mary were married. If you want a good secretary get a Virgo girl. There is a characteristic Virgo tenseness which can often result in constipation.

The sign was symbolized by the virgin. Sex is not the same to these people as to the more emotional signs. They are practical people. They may be too concerned with the practical ramifications of sex to ever enjoy it.

They are not easily aroused. Instead, they are thinking about rules and regulations. They'd probably rather talk about it. After all, it is something to talk about. Of course, if they are convinced that this is what people do, then they must do what people do. The problem is how to be a member of society and do what the *best* people of society expect of one. It is difficult for them to cut themselves away from the past. They have good memories about it. Sticking to the rules and the routine doesn't bother Virgo very much, but can drive Gemini crazy. Virgo can make a great proofreader. The sign won't miss a mistake. They may enjoy crossword puzzles. In mathematics, the sign represents the accountant rather than the man who understands abstract mathematics and digs out formulas, but Virgo can look them up in a book and apply them. Again, there is practicality. Virgo wants things to work on the material plane. Gemini does too, but not enough to stay with it and frustrate himself.

Virgo is more money-conscious. It likes bargains, and could often become a sucker for one. Values are values, but Virgo thinks in terms of material values, what it costs elsewhere. The Virgo wife might spend more on gasoline than she saves by checking everybody's prices.

Virgo can tolerate routine, while Gemini can dislike it. The result is that Virgo is likely to be much more tidy than Gemini. Virgo is much more concerned with what other people think. Gemini will listen to what others think but won't be concerned about it. It will listen because of curiosity. Virgo sees cause in matter. Gemini sees cause in ideas. As a rule, Gemini will see the humorous or ridiculous side of things, while Virgo will see the more serious side. Gemini can better stand periods of isolation or seclusion. These are both mental signs, but a different kind of mentality. On the average, the Virgo wife will keep the better household, may protect her husband's interests better and may be considered more "faithful," but the Gemini wife will be more interesting, and will have a better sense of humor. She can be flippant and amusing, but the beds may not have been made. Remember, there are exceptions to these rules, but they will work on the average. Compare ten Virgo housewives with ten Gemini housewives, and see what you get.

Among the men of these two signs, we do not particularly find the executive type. Gemini isn't particularly interested in ruling over others. The Virgo man needs somebody behind him to make some of the decisions and back him up. A good Virgo executive has to have something else in his horoscope. Lyndon Johnson was born with the Sun in Virgo, but it was conjunct with the executive Mars, ruler of Scorpio. Gemini is more intuitive than Virgo. William Howard Taft was a Virgo President. His son, Senator Robert Taft, was also

Virgo. Gemini men often make very good lawyers. They are expert at arguing or debating either side of a case. A Virgo can get buried in the letter of the law, while a Gemini can go all around it with his own interpretations, mix up and confuse a jury and then win it over to his side. His personality will be likely to have more appeal for a jury. Virgo may prepare a case better. Perhaps a Gemini lawyer should have a Virgo assistant before going into the court room, or have Virgo at his elbow during the trial. Gemini doesn't have the organizing ability of Virgo. In fact, he may be more at home with a bit of confusion.

One of the best and most successful astrologers of this century, Grant Lewi, was a Gemini, but he was noted most for his writings on the subject. Before he became an astrologer, he taught English. Whenever he made a business or financial success, he got bored with it and went on to something that would be more challenging. He liked to move around and be going some place. His humor was always preceded by the twinkle in his eye.

CHAPTER VI

Taurus and Libra

(Taurus Born April 20th through May 19th.
Libra Born September 23rd through October 22nd.)

Taurus and Libra are usually friendly and perhaps lethargic signs. They are strongly attracted to the opposite sex but are not particularly aggressive about it. They are more inclined to let things come to them. They would rather entertain at home than go visiting. They would prefer to attract people to themselves than run after them. Yet, here we have some very romantic people. They react more than they initiate. Both signs can be very much attached to their homes. These are not what we could call the nervous types, particularly Taurus is not. In fact, it can be stoic. Neither sign is too easily aroused. They are more inclined to take things in their stride. You can't easily know what they are think-ing because they don't react easily. They are much more calm than other signs. They appear to be more easily satisfied. For all of this, for all of these similarities, they are opposites in many respects.

Taurus is more material. It comes into the world to think of and deal with material things, but under certain conditions is capable of great transformations. It likes the land and likes it in big quantities. William Randolph Hearst, with his big California ranch plus the biggest ranch in Mexico where he maintained for years a stronger force of men than the Mexican government, was a Taurean. William Myron Keck, who founded Superior Oil Company and ran up a personal fortune of hundreds of millions of dollars, was a Taurean. When he died, there was $17 million in his personal bank ac-counts. This sign runs way above average among bank-ers and Wall Street men. The Keck estate was actually bigger than that of Hearst. Keck's Superior Oil stock, which sold for 20 cents in 1930, sold for over $2000 a share in the 1960's. In other words, great wealth is often connected with this sign. These people often build up great power of one kind or another. They enjoy pos-sessing great power, even if they never use it. Hitler was a Taurean and a mark against the sign. We had a break-through of a Taurean into the metaphysical in Shake-speare. In the entertainment world, Bing Crosby and

Jack Paar are Taureans. So was Lionel Barrymore. Taurean women, for the most part, are inclined to be settled. They can get pretty attached to their homes and families. They can be very steadying influences upon their husbands. They will enjoy entertaining at home, but they like good homes in which to entertain.

Libra isn't so attached to material things above what they may need for comfort. They like nice things and appreciate quality. They would prefer to do their entertaining in a small way with a select group of friends. They are less impressed by bigness. They don't concentrate on one thing the way a Taurean will. There is stubbornness in Taurus, but this is rare in Libra. When enthused, Taurus has a one-track mind, one objective upon which it concentrates to the seclusion of all else. Libra is not like that. It weighs both sides of any subject. It knows when something is off balance. The symbol of Taurus was the bull (In America, the stagg), and of Libra the scales of balance and justice. Except when the ruling planet, Venus, is in Scorpio, Libra can be a very just sign. It doesn't want to hurt anybody. There is a considerable difference in that Taurus believes in its own power even thought it is a cautious sign, while Libra lacks self-confidence. You have to convince Libra how good it is. Try to tell Libra how good it is and it will appreciate it, but probably won't believe it. Nevertheless, the sign will feel good because you said so. Too few Libra people develop their talents properly because of the lack of self-confidence. There is often good musical or artistic ability that is not developed. The sign likes all flattery even if it doesn't believe it. Flattery will make these people think you like them, and they will be happy about that.

There is an ability to understand abstract design, with the result that Libra can become a masterful mathematician if the fear of mathematics as a subject is overcome. That is not the fault of Libra. It is the fault of the way the subject has been taught. Down through centuries, it has been made forbidding in order to exaggerate the ability of those teaching it. It is apt to flatter Libra to be desired sexually, and the sign can be very affectionate. While Taurus can be sluggish until it gets started or gets up its momentum, Libra is inclined to be lazy. The women enjoy sweets, and if contentedly married, they can become compulsive eaters. Then weight becomes a problem. Doctors investigating the subject find more Libra women afflicted with obesity than any other sign. They need a new interest of some kind to make them forget foods and sweets. With Libra, the kidneys can be a weak spot, while with Taurus it is the throat.

Libra doesn't usually have the staying power of Taurus. It is interesting to note that some of the longest books, particularly books on technical or scientific subjects, are written by Taureans. Some of them are pretty dogmatic. We might mention long books written by Carl Marx, Hitler, Sigmund Freud, Herbert Spencer, Lester Ward, Emmanuel Kant and Spinoza—all Taureans. Offhand, we can't think of a long technical book written by a Libran.

Neither of these signs can ordinarily be called impulsive. They don't usually take the initiative. They wait till they see how things are going. If they are going all right, there will be no need to do anything about it. Yet, many of the greatest military men have been born under these signs. They are not warriors. They do not want to fight, but if somebody is going to fight, they'll be likely to withdraw until they develop or assemble sufficient strength to win. U. S. Grant was a Taurean.

It is more difficult for Taurus to break away from the hereditary factor than for Libra to do so. There is basic family loyalty in Taurus, but if Libra doesn't like its relatives, it will look elsewhere for friends to take the place of relatives. It may show more interest in strangers than Taurus.

Neither of these signs is insecure insofar as material things are concerned, but Libra can be personally insecure. There can be an inferiority complex. This can be overcome if Libra can be shown how much talent it actually has. It must learn how to use it and apply it. A few good loyal friends can do much for the Libra personality. In most instances, both signs are inclined to be reliable, but there can be some marked exceptions to this rule. Friends can mean a great deal to both signs. They enjoy having good friends. Taurus may be inclined to surround itself with friends who are well fixed financially, while to Libra, this wouldn't be such a consideration where friends are concerned. Many other factors would be more important. Libra is actually a more intellectual sign than Taurus. It can better deal with abstractions and abstract principles.

Neither of these signs can be considered as aggressive, nor can we call them ambitious signs. The Taureans who are ready to push themselves almost invariably have planets in Aries also (like Hitler), while the Librans who will push themselves seem to have planets in Scorpio. Otherwise, that push isn't there. Vitality and ambition are lacking. These are not ordinarily to be considered signs of self-interest. They will usually step aside for others. It isn't their nature to step on other people's toes. If they don't like a person, they will stay away from that person. They won't annoy him. When they can have harmonious associations they will be very cooperative. They are slow to anger, but don't push them too far. Particularly Taurus can be extremely violent if pushed too far. It is said he is then like the bull in a china shop. As we come to the combination of Aries and Scorpio, you will see a marked difference in basic character structure.

CHAPTER VII

Aries and Scorpio

(Aries Born March 21st through April 19th.
Scorpio Born October 23rd through November 21st.)

Aries and Scorpio were known as the Mars sign. Both signs have a relationship with Mars and Pluto, but Mars rules Scorpio, while Pluto rules Aries. These are the aggressive, impulsive but executive signs. They are alike and yet they are different.

Family or group loyalty is characteristic of Scorpio, while Aries is more individualistic, independent, daring and venturesome. Scorpio must be a part of something, while Aries must lead or go it alone. Both signs have drive, but Scorpio's is an emotional drive while the drive of Aries is vital and from the spirit. Aries initiates while Scorpio reacts. Aries can burn but Scorpio can boil.

Aries is the natural pioneer. It can survive alone if necessary. Otherwise, it must have a following. It isn't good at being a follower. Particularly business pioneers come out of this sign. A large ratio of the Taureans who have become pioneers actually had a flock of planets in Aries, and this was their motivating force. John Hays Hammond was an Aries. He pioneered the West and built his mining empire. His son, John Hays Hammond Jr. was also born to Aries. He pioneered electronics, the house trailer and many other things and built a greater fortune. Aries does not do as well in politics, although Thomas Jefferson, left his mark, but witness the briefer stay of other Aries men Harold Stassen and Dean Acheson. We have not elected an Aries president since John Tyler in 1840. The only other one we ever did elect was Jefferson in 1800, but we kept him for two terms. Few Aries men can adapt themselves to modern politics, where the president waits to see what the public wants before letting anyone know where he stands. Aries would have its own ideas of what the public needs and would want to see that people got it. The modern public probably wouldn't ever understand a good Aries president like Jefferson. Aries does best in business and when running his own business. He would be happier as president of a small business than as vice-president of a large business. He needs an opportunity to express his own creative nature. He doesn't do as well working under other people. Consider people from the early movie world, Mary Pickford, her husband Douglas Fairbanks and Charles Chaplin. They were original. Jefferson's ideas about democracy were also original.

By contrast, consider Scorpio as seen in Theodore Roosevelt, Senator Robert Kennedy, Warren G. Harding, James Knox Polk, James Garfield. Although he originated much, Theodore Roosevelt was always very conscious of what the common man wanted.

Scorpio cannot be the lone wolf as Aries can. He needs company. He is close to his family, loyal to his heredity, as well as to those above him or those beneath him. He believes in working as a team. He is wary of the stranger and may consider him a potential enemy. He has a suspicious nature and is always alert for the possibility of a betrayal. He expects those around him to be loyal to him too. His feelings are badly hurt if others do not stand by him.

The ancients associated Scorpio with sex and gave it the symbol of the Scorpion. Aries was the ram with its head and horns down. Sex is a strong factor in the Scorpio individual, but it can also be associated with a guilt complex. We find the Scorpio minister out preaching against sin (Billy Sunday and Billy Graham). Scorpio produces many of the best executives. They are loyal to the people for whom they work. They inspire loyalty on the part of those who work under them.

They are secretive when secrecy is needed. They can delegate authority. They are always on the job. They know what is going on everywhere. They concentrate on making the business successful.

The Scorpio woman has sex as a motivation force. She is more likely to have health problems that relate to the female organs. At least in this writer's experience, he has run up against more cases of young Scorpio girls who became pregnant before marriage than girls of any other sign. Sex can be a difficult factor for Scorpio people because it is such a powerful factor with these people. It is always with them. On the unconscious level, they are trying to perpetuate their heredity by having children, and yet, after the act is over, they have that feeling of guilt, but they can have guilt feelings about many other things too. The sign is emotional and impulsive, but it is the first to feel sorry for any mistakes it has made. It will sincerely want to rectify any wrong. On the other hand, it can hold a grudge, and it does not forgive a wrong easily. Both Scorpio and Aries are more accident-prone than other signs, but Aries has a habit of sustaining injuries to the head. Scorpio seems to have more surgery than the average of the other signs.

Because of her individuality, the Aries woman might find it more difficult to bow to the will of her husband, but she can usually be pretty diplomatic about that because she wants her husband. He is a basic part of her domain, but indirectly, she will probably control the domain, including her husband. In effect, he will be one of the children, but he may need more attention to keep him under control. Aries women are usually very artful at this.

It is surprising what a high ratio of Aries people of both sexes can have problems relating to children. There can be many health problems involving the children, and Aries is inclined to do all the children's thinking for them, sometimes to the extent of selecting their careers for them. They should be ultra careful that they do not, in this way, drive their own children away from them when they become adults. The motion picture, *Sign of the Ram*, had this theme. Another odd thing about the natives of Aries is that they seem to be very lucky at gambling, taking chances, etc. This can reverse itself if Pluto, ruler of Aries, was in affliction at the time of birth. If you want to tabulate the health problems of enough of these two groups of people, it won't take you too long to determine why the ancients associated Aries with the head and Scorpio with the sex organs.

Will power is one of the strong features of Aries. It is capable of fighting off great physical pain, and will not give in to pain easily. Aries can often fight off disease by sheer will power. Another sign couldn't do it. Aries intends to be master of its own destiny. Unlike the Taurus-Libra group, it doesn't wait for opportunity to come along. It goes after it. Aries is the promoter, and a good one. A very high ratio of these people are attracted to horses and horse races. An Aries woman of this writer's acquaintance won three daily doubles in California in one week. It sounds impossible, but it happened. This writer knows a whole group of Aries housewives who are consistently winning prizes in raffles. The Aries man will almost root the horse he has bet upon into the lead. That Aries will is something more than imagination.

There is nothing lethargic about either of these signs. They are always active. There is plenty to do and they are doing it. They can accomplish an enormous amount of work, whether it is physical or another kind. They live in the present, although Aries may have its mind somewhat on the future, and Scorpio is not entirely free of the past. This has more to do with the unconscious realms, however. Consciously, both will be living the NOW. Aries isn't bothered by the past the way so many people are, because of its conviction that it is going to make the future what it wants it to be—and a lot better. Aside from all else, Aries needs its hobbies. Another characteristic difference between Aries and Scorpio is that Scorpio cannot hide its feelings. The sign is too emotional for that, but Aries can completely conceal what its feelings really are. It is too proud to allow other people to know it can be hurt. It is not inclined to let other people know it needs them. It can always find a way of going it alone if necessary, and in that way preserve its pride. Its strength comes from inside, while Scorpio draws its strength from others, in some cases to the extent of becoming a psychic vampire. Aries finds it easy to break away from its heredity, while Scorpio is the reverse. Aries may break away from the family early in order to get started producing its own family which it will own by itself. Its own family is the new world. Aries is more likely to marry into a different kind of heredity, and to marry into a different race or religion. Scorpio is more apt to marry someone who resembles a member of his own family. The Scorpio woman is likely to worship her father and marry some man who looks like him or resembles him in some other way. Despite their own strong wills, Aries will not encourage the same strong wills in their own children. Perhaps one such will in a family is sufficient. Don't forget that no person is all one sign. There are usually mixtures of signs.

CHAPTER VIII

Pisces and Sagittarius

*(Pisces Born February 19th through March 20th.
Sagittarius Born November 22nd through December 21st.)*

We related Gemini and Virgo to the nervous system. Pisces and Sagittarius are related to something beyond the nervous system, which is in some way connected to it. These signs relate to some of the phenomenon that orthodox science and the academicians are afraid to investigate. The psychic powers are related to Pisces, while intuition is related to Sagittarius. Pisces is ruled by Neptune, Sagittarius by Jupiter. Both of these signs have a strong curiosity about the unknown and something akin to a religious interest, although it may not be a church type of interest. The consciousness of both signs goes beyond the usual, everyday affairs of life. Survival and money-making isn't enough. People born under these signs are not materialists. They are less inclined to live according to rules and regulations. They are not at all inclined to be atheists. They are less likely to doubt life after death or existence in some form prior to his life. They both recognize the vastness of the unknown, and are less likely to accept what the authorities say about it. Both signs like to travel and explore. Yet, in other respects, these two signs are the opposite of each other.

Sagittarius is direct and to the point. People born under the sign are outspoken. They say what they think regardless, usually without stopping to consider what the consequences might be. This is plain, simple honesty, the sort of thing society requests but can't take. Most of the German spies caught in this country during World War II were Sagittarians. They were, not because Germany was selecting Sagittarians as spies in foreign countries but, because they spoke out of turn. After succeeding in getting into the country, they had to brag and sing the praises of Hitler. This brought them attention they would not have otherwise received and not the type of attention they were seeking. This is an optimistic sign as a rule, unless there are planets in Capricorn, next to it. There is great faith in the protective power of some entity greater than self. Sagittarians are natural crusaders. They go out and fight for what they believe in. The one astrology magazine with an undisguised religious slant, *Astrology Guide*, is edited by a Sagittarian, Dal Lee. Yet, the philosophical outlook of the Sagittarian is in a constant state of evolution. Seldom do we find one of these people who remains within the church in which he was brought up. These people are not easily brainwashed. The desire of a Sagittarian to learn the truth is much more powerful than his loyalty to any church or to his family or heredity. These people are interested in almost all branches of knowledge—anything that has something to do with the hidden truth. Whether they do or do not obtain an orthodox education, these natives will keep looking further and further into the unknown. They have very strong intuition, particularly when they need it for some reason. If Jupiter was well aspected and conditioned, the more so. Experiments of the writer indicated that of all signs, this sign is the best at guessing the cards in ESP (extrasensory perception) tests. Dr. Charles Stuart, a mathematician at Duke University, was tops at such guessing. He was co-author of one of Dr. J. B. Rhine's books. The average Sagittarian is more jovial than other signs. If you need help, he won't walk by. If you are down, he will want to cheer you up, and he may then try to indoctrinate you with his philosophy, not to indoctrinate you, but to cheer you up and give you a better, more optimistic outlook, because a good outlook can be vital.

Pisces is the opposite of Sagittarius in many respects. In place of intuition, it is likely to have psychic powers. It may dream events before they happen. It lives partly in some other, unknown world. It can have mental and emotional problems that Sagittarius is not likely to know about unless it has some very negative Neptunian afflictions. In place of outspokenness, Pisces is secretive. Instead of wanting to tell the truth, it will tell what it thinks will have the best effect upon you, or the effect that it desires. For this reason, the sign develops some of the best public relations people, or the ones who have been most desired during recent times. Nobody ever knows just what the Pisces person thinks, because it never tells its true thoughts to anyone, not because it thinks its thoughts are wrong, but because it knows that society is too brainwashed to be able to face the truth. It is interesting to note what happens when you get both of these signs involved in one chart. Tiffany Thayer had Sun-in-Pisces, with Sagittarius rising. In the 1920's he was one of the first daring sex writers with a sense of humor. Later, he ran the magazine *Doubt* of the Fortian Society. In fact, he started the Fortian Society. In one way, he was outspoken. In another way, he was secretive and never expressed just what he did believe. He was a pal of the great. One moment, he would shock you with his unorthodox ideas. The next moment, he would appear to conform, to find out what your ideas were. If he found you interesting, you would find him quite silent, but he would keep opening more bottles of imported wines. He would encourage you to go on. L. Ron Hubbard was also a combination of these two signs. Here was another crusader. He began by writing science-fiction, but wound up founding both Dianetics and Scientology. Note that both these men produced best-selling books. Both were interested in bringing forth the truth. Both were outspoken in saying what was more-or-less forbidden by social codes, but also note they are really mystics. Each traveled widely, but there is left the impression that both men kept much knowledge to themselves. Both of them were married a number of times. Both of them spent much time in England. Thayer was a close friend of Bertrand Russell, and would go to England just to visit with him. Russell was also a free-thinker. All three took exception to religious dogma pertaining to sex. This writer had the privilege of knowing Thayer intimately, Hubbard by correspondence. At one time, this writer dined once a week with Thayer in a tavern on Third Avenue. There was a rule. If we were free on a certain night of the week, we would be at the tavern.

Sagittarius was portrayed and symbolized by the ancients, always with arrows. In Europe, there was the centaur with drawn bow and arrow. In the American pre-Spanish zodiacs, there were always arrows, regardless of the rest of the portrayal. We ordinarily associate the bow and arrow with the American Indian. How did it find its way into zodiacs coming out of northern Africa? Did Africans and American Indians invent it independently, and if they did, why did they both associate it with Sagittarius?

Consider the symbol in the Bible. In Revelations 6:2, we are told, "And I saw, and behold, a white horse, and he that sat thereon had a bow . . ." Revelations is filled with astrological symbolism. The second horse is red (associated with Mars, but correctly with Pluto), and "to him that sat thereon, it was given to take peace from the earth" (the god of war—Mars or Pluto). With regard to the third horse, "a Black horse, and he that sat thereon had a balance in his hand (Libra and the scales of justice)."

To one familiar with astrological symbolism, it is obvious that all the religions originated out of astrology, but it is doubtful whether any of them have been understood during modern times—in the last 1900 years. This is one of the things Sir Isaac Newton wrote about, but publication of his writings was forbidden by the Church of England and the so-called *scientists* of England.

Pisces was always portrayed with fish, the European

symbol being two fish swimming in opposite directions, yet tied together by reeds. It was a symbol of confusion. Pisces can be confused because it lives in two different worlds. If it told all, it would be thrown into a mental institution or a jail—and sometimes is. Yet, it produces the greatest of genius. Luther Burbank talked to his flowers to encourage them to grow and bloom . . . and they did. George Washington, who was subtle enough to know how to fight the Indians in their own way, was Pisces. This is the sign of the mystic. It is just as sexual as Scorpio, but in a different way. Scorpio can be sadistic, while Pisces is the masochist . . . It doesn't resist sex. Albert Einstein was Pisces. He said that he didn't think God threw dice, meaning that he did not really believe in the accepted theory of mathematical probability. He had some other idea, but he was subtle. He didn't say what it was. In their own way, both Burbank and Einstein were mystics. If you are a true mystic, you don't advertise it. Either *science* or the church might burn you at the stake.

As a rule, the Sagittarian woman has a good figure and takes sex in her stride, seeing much that is funny about it. The Pisces woman just takes it, often as much as she can get of it. It is something that she isn't likely to resist. Pisces recognizes that most moral codes are strictly phoney and born of hypocrisy. The sign doesn't try to change them. It recognizes that hypocrisy is characteristic of the human species. It goes around the codes and does what it wishes to do secretly. It doesn't crusade to change the laws as Sagittarius does. Sagittarius is too apt to mistake hypocrisy for ignorance. It can't really believe that human nature is dishonest, because its own nature is not dishonest. While Sagittarius would not make a good spy in a foreign country, Pisces would do better, because it can keep a secret. It won't talk out of turn—or is not as likely to. Like Sagittarius, Pisces can have a good sense of humor, but it is likely to be a very subtle sense of humor. These people are sympathetic and compassionate. They feel for the unfortunate. They will care for the sick and the injured. They recognize the criminal as a sick person and believe he should be treated in a hospital instead of being punished. Warden Lawes of Sing Sing Prison, the great prison reformer, was a Pisces. Drugs and alcohol are often associated with Pisces. The sign can consume a great deal of alcohol without becoming an alcoholic. In fact, many Pisces seem to thrive on alcohol without finding it injurious. Scorpio is more apt to become an alcoholic, perhaps because of guilt. Pisces is unlikely to have any guilt. Whatever it may do, it doesn't have any feeling that it is wrong. After all, what can be wrong in what Pisces does, when the rest of the world is so hypocritical and when it raises other beings such as sheep and cattle, merely to cannibalistically devour them? In its own way, Pisces is a type of moralist. Its heart goes out to the lower beings, the ones who are really being abused. It doesn't believe God is so sadistic as to approve of the moral codes of modern society.

CHAPTER IX

Aquarius and Capricorn

(Aquarius Born January 20th through February 18th.
Capricorn Born December 22nd through January 19th.)

Astrology associates Capricorn with the planet Saturn, Aquarius with the planet Uranus. It is very easy for people with the Sun in one of these signs to have planets in the other, since the two signs join, one following the other. In that case, you get a mixed type. Basically, Capricorn is trying to protect the established order, while Aquarius is attempting to change it. This is a battle that goes on forever. We see it in politics and government. We see it on the home front. There is always the question, "Is it time for a change?" Capricorn is the conservative, Aquarius the progressive (not the Liberal as we know him. The Liberal is more likely to be associated with Pisces and Neptune).

Capricorn people are often a frustrated people. They are apt to be more successful in earlier than in later life, because they get along better with older persons, accept authority, and do what is expected of them by the previous generation. When the older people have died out, they are licked, and they do not understand the attitude of younger folks. They are likely to live in the past. They think in terms of the good old days. They worship their ancestors like the old orientals. The young Capricorn usually gets along very well with his parents and is very much attached to them. He looks to them for guidance. He tolerates frustrations. In fact, he frustrates himself. He is very practical in his ideas. Unless born to wealth, he isn't likely to get married too early because he doesn't see how he can support a wife and family. It is surprising how often a Capricorn man marries a professional woman who can support herself. Capricorn women will marry principally to improve their economic status—not for love. She'll take the money and then frustrate herself for the rest of her life. Capricorn people are that insecure about material things. They don't want any trouble. They don't believe in taking any unnecessary chances. They will put up with a great deal for the sake of material security. Capricorn assumes responsibility in what Aquarius would consider an unnecessary way. There are always those periodic trips to see old aunt Minnie. Aunt Minnie is pretty old, and she isn't going to live forever, and there is that farm. She will have to leave it to someone. Capricornians don't like change. It makes them feel insecure. Why aren't people ever satisfied? This sign thinks age and wisdom are synonymous. Often, these people seem to select the hardest kind of work for themselves. If born on a farm, they will stick with the farm. It will be a sad day when the children want to leave the farm. A true Capricornian seldom leaves his place of birth, but there are such mixed types.

Barry Goldwater is a mixed type. He has the Sun in Capricorn and considers himself a conservative. He has the Sun conjunct with Uranus, ruler of Aquarius. Had he been a true conservative, he would have stayed in Phoenix, and would have had no desire to go to Washington. He has Sagittarius at the Ascendent at birth, so he is also the crusader. Different people see different phases of Goldwater, and nobody ever seems to see all of him, unless familiar with his horoscope.

A true Capricorn conservative wouldn't be likely to get into politics in the first place, except perhaps at the home level. Consequently, those who do get into politics in a bigger way are usually part Aquarius. Woodrow Wilson and Alfred E. Smith were both men with Sun in Capricorn, but each had Aquarius on the Ascendant at birth. People with Aquarius on the Ascendant at birth usually have a very long face, and a long nose. Note what a high ratio of such faces you see on television. You can always learn more about these two types by studying the two together. Their interests are the same, but their views about those interests are in reverse. Capricorn wants to uphold the constitution. Capricorn wants to see that the laws are upheld, while Aquarius wants to change them. We satisfy both groups by passing new laws while leaving the old laws on the books. We just don't enforce the old laws any more, except to persecute somebody.

Aquarius sees into the future because it is the future and not the past which interests him. After all, he is interested in where he is going, not where he has been. He leaves the past behind him and forgets about it, while Capricorn can never forget the past. Aquarius completely forgets that he had an Aunt Minnie, but Aunt Minnie doesn't forget him. She sees his picture in the newspapers, and she reads about him. She is very proud of him, and tells all her neighbors about her nephew. Capricorn is a good boy, but he isn't like her Aquarius nephew who is famous. Even if he became famous by merely robbing a bank, his picture was in the newspaper. He always was an interesting child. He'll get out of this mess. He always does. Jimmy Hoffa is an Aquarian.

Divorce is common among Aquarians, uncommon among Capricornians, unless the mate brings it about. Capricorn will stick it out. To the Aquarian, the mate is associated with a past interval and doesn't fit the new cycle coming up. Aquarius has great curiosity, is an abstractionist, less interested in material things, and has great inventive ability. These people like change. The new and different are always fascinating. There is alertness toward all progress and change. Aquarius likes excitement. They like to see things happen in a big way, perhaps a big electrical storm, a riot, or the dropping of an atomic bomb. Aquarius doesn't fear the future the way Capricorn does. The sign has more confidence, and the past seems so dull now that anything would be better than that. There is great curiosity about the unknown. Aquarius is more open-minded and considers all possibilities. It is better prepared to meet whatever comes along because it has not already decided that the future will be just like the past. It assumes and hopes that the future will be a surprise, so that when it is a surprise, Aquarius reacts automatically, and knows what to do about it. It thinks quickly about being an opportunist in taking advantage of the new situation, while Capricorn must first get over the shock, before being able to even think about what it is to do now. The

Aquarian is more of a hobo in nature, and there are advantages in the hobo philosophy.

Aquarius is more likely to be successful in later life, because it has always been ahead of its time. Abraham Lincoln was an Aquarian, but it was over 100 years after his death that the world began carrying out some of his ideas relating to the Negro. Franklin D. Roosevelt was an Aquarian, and when the country finally made up its mind to have a big change, he was ready to bring it about. Born on the exact same day and year as Lincoln, Charles Darwin presented us with the first views of evolution, and the first suspicion indicating that perhaps the story of creation given in Genesis should not be taken literally. This was a shock to organized society. As late as 1925, the State of Tennessee was prosecuting John T. Scopes for teaching evolution in conflict with the fundamentalist Biblical interpretation. It remains against the law to teach evolution in Tennessee, so Saturn and Capricorn must remain in control down there. They don't enforce the law, but they keep it on the books. They might want to persecute someone.

Thomas Edison was an Aquarian. To get an idea across, he had to light one district of New York City free of charge in order to demonstrate the value of electric lights. He also gave us moving pictures and the phonograph which ultimately developed into the modern talking movie and all of our voice recording gadgets. When some great change is brought about in the world and the old traditions, conventions, fetishes, rules and regulations are dropped, it is usually an Aquarian who brings it about, but he must first overcome all the mass, inertia, gravity and fixity of Capricorn and Saturn.

The Aquarius woman is not about to fit herself into the ancient order of things, even if her Capricorn sister is willing to frustrate herself. A true Capricorn man would have a difficult time trying to keep up with an Aquarian wife. She likes freedom. She will come and go pretty much as she pleases. She isn't much on routine. Whatever she did yesterday, it must be different tomorrow. She lives in a state of evolution. She is always evolving. Whatever she thinks today will be different tomorrow, because she has learned more by plunging further into the unknown. Her husband will probably tolerate it all, but he will forever wonder why she is not satisfied, why she doesn't finally settle into a state of inertia for, to him, true inertia is the ultimate happiness. To her, inertia and death are synonymous. Male or female, Aquarians probably marry more times in one life than any other sign. It's part of their evolution. That's the way you get to learn and know about people, and find out what they are like. How can a woman learn all about men from one husband? The divorce rate seems far higher among Aquarians than among Capricornians, particularly among Aquarians who are not in public life and do not have to put up a false front to avoid the horrification of a hypocritical society with all of its hypocritical religious leanings. The Aquarian is always moving on into new territory.

CHAPTER X

How Much Is Predictable?

As this chapter is being written on August 15th, 1965, blood is running in the streets of Los Angeles. Twenty-two are dead. Many are wounded. Property damage is in the millions. Newspapers are calling it the *Battle of Los Angeles*. Meanwhile and simultaneously, the National Guard has been called out in Chicago, where rioting is the "worst in twelve years." Could all of this have been predicted?

From page 49 of Volume 1, Number of 5 of *Borderline* magazine:

The year 1965 will be one of the most emotional we have ever experienced. Racial problems can grow worse. Blood could run in the streets. Sex problems will mount, and mental illness, along with violent crimes, will reach a new high, as a result of conflict and confusion. Youth will be crusading . . . Stocks will be erratic . . . When people are under emotional stress, they follow patterns of emotional behavior, and under this kind of a design, they become violent . . . It can also mean uncontrolled, out-of-hand, mob violence. The mob doesn't think. It feels and it acts.

Note that the rioters were young people and children. The Dow-Jones averages broke 100 points. These were not the first riots. There had been serious riots in Harlem, Rochester, Philadelphia and elsewhere in 1964, but 1965 was much worse. However, this writer began warnings two years before, back in early 1963, when he wrote:

There is going to be a surplus of human energy. Society must become conscious of this, and be prepared to direct it into constructive channels. Otherwise it will result in juvenile and adult delinquency. The downtrodden and ignored will revolt and will fight, and will destroy. Unless society is going to meet its responsibilities toward the unfortunate and under-privileged, it will have rebellion and insurrection on its hands.

In making these predictions, which were based on the conjunction of Uranus and Pluto, a very rare conjunction which had not occurred since the year 1851 before

Pluto was even discovered, the writer had merely gone back to see what was happening in 1851 and the years leading up to it. There were similar riots caused by children in those days. On November 20th, 1851, 45 pupils were killed and 60 were injured in a panic at Public School 26 in New York City. There were many other riots accompanied by the spilling of blood. The Uranus-Pluto conjunction lasts several years, and 34 persons had been killed in the Astor Place riots of 1849.

The riots and insurrection of 1964 and 1965 were well predicted by astrology. The conjunction of Uranus-Pluto is not complete, and it extends into 1966 and could even have some effects in 1967. This prediction involved mob psychology, about which psychologists should know something, but note that psychologists have *never* been able to *predict* human behavior or mob psychology, while astrology does. Actually, the first psychologists were astrologers, and they are still the best psychologists. Let the psychologists go back over the writer's public predictions and try to find him wrong. The psychologists do not even have hopes of ultimately duplicating these accomplishments, and yet, the academicians put all of their faith in psychology rather than in astrology.

However, let's not allow these predictions to give us an inaccurate outlook. Predictions have to be within the limitation of what we know. There are some astrologers who have gone on record with a lot of predictions that were wrong, but this was the fault of the astrologer, not of astrology. A mathematician can make a mistake in his figures and come up with the wrong answer, but that does not prove nor indicate that mathematics was wrong. Over the 35 years this writer has been writing on astrology, he has been overly cautious not to go into print unless he was certain of what he was saying. The reader should be very careful not to overestimate the ability of this writer or any other astrologer. Just as important as what we can predict is what we cannot predict, and there is much that we cannot predict. What is needed is an accurate appraisal of what we *can* and *cannot* predict. There are many things the writer would like to predict for himself, but he can't.

We can predict enough to prove that astrology can work, but what is lacking is sufficient research. Much of what has been passed down by the ancients has been completely distorted or misinterpreted by the moderns. Astrology is not a religion any more than mathematics is a religion, but we have the lunatic fringe always either seeking a savior or trying to be one, and this fringe has proven very unreliable. It has done astrology much harm in the public eye, but we must not condemn it too much because without it, astrology would never have been preserved at all. We do have the lunatic fringe among astrologers, but it is not as great as the lunatic fringe among astronomers and other academicians. The dangerous thing is that the lunatic fringe among the academicians is allowed by the universities and other educational institutions of the country to be presented under the disguise of *science*. It is a means of completely fooling and brainwashing our modern youth. It is our worst form of insanity. It is unrelated to true science, which is supposedly concerned with truth, accuracies and the factual.

A small handfull of people have contributed to astrological research. We can mention Vernon Clark, Ernest A. Grant and Grath Allen among the few who have done any actual statistical research. There has been other work that we will not mention here because if too few cases were not involved, the mathematical systems employed were questionable. The writer cannot mention the names of three men in Wall Street who contributed to his research back in 1940. His earlier work was financed by *American Astrology Magazine*. This work necessitated the indexing of over 100,000 birthdates. In actual cash, the writer's research received its greatest support from Kenneth Greenwood, a retired engineer of Tucson. Like the rest of us, Charles A. Jayne tried but didn't find much in the way of support.

There is now a group of 30 or more doctors of the country engaged in such statistical research, and the size of the group is growing, but none of the work has yet been published. They have three years of work behind them since the group was originally organized in the writer's hotel room at the Chicago Sheraton Hotel back in 1962.

Astrology needs millions of dollars for research, but billions of dollars are being given to less important work in other fields, mainly attempting to prove unprovable theories and hypotheses in order to uphold and support our modern academic world or sophisticated dogma. Almost all current research has as its basic purpose to try and support and uphold unproved doctrine of materialism which holds that all cause lies in matter. Research funds in the space program appear to have been better administered with less dogma and prejudice. Astrology has had to face the professional jealousy of the astronomers, some of the psychologists, the phycisists, some members of the clergy and the academicians in general. Here is the richest field on earth for research today, but millions of dollars plus the proper administration is necessary. The time has not yet come. It will, but when? That is one more thing the writer would like to be able to predict but can't. Charles Fort said, "You steamboat when comes steamboat time." Not before that. You could never have sold Ford cars to the ancient Greeks. It would have been too soon.

It is probably true that modern astrology offers more

knowledge on marriage, love and sex problems than in any other realm. There is a reason for this. This is the type of problem that brings people to astrologers. We have the factor of supply and demand. The astrologer has been able to spend more money on research in connection with sex and astrology than in any other field, because the money to support such research is more available. Money, health and other problems may take people to astrologers, but not in the manner that sex problems do. In this field, one astrologer can tell a client more about a sex problem than all the doctors and psychologists in the country, unless it happens to be a purely physical rather than a psychological or emotional problem.

Don't underestimate what astrology and astrologers can do, but on the other hand, don't overestimate what they can do.

Astrology has never taught fatalism as astronomers and clergymen are prone to assume without investigating the subject. The poets have probably left this impression. There are many things we predict daily without giving them much thought. We predict the sunrise, the approximate temperature and weather, the time a train or a plane will leave or arrive, the time of the new or the full moon, when summer or winter will be here, the approximate number of deaths over a holiday weekend, etc. Not all of these predictions are right, but a high ratio of them are. A plane may crash before it arrives, not very often, but occasionally. Another may not depart on time because of a storm. The weather bureau may go all wrong at times, be fairly accurate at other times.

The most accurate predictions are those based on the mathematics of the solar system, the sunrise, the new or full moon, eclipses, etc. The space age has taught us much that we did not know a few years back. Suppose we became able to build a tremendous thrust power far beyond anything we know today. Suppose it employed atomic power. By setting it off at just the right time at just the right place, with the thrust pointed away from the earth instead of toward its center, it would be possible to slow down the earth's rotation. Or perhaps speed it up. Or we might change the earth's orbit. This would change the time of sunrise or sunset. It might completely change the seasons. It might completely change the temperature of the earth. An error might plunge the earth into the fires of the sun. Many things could happen.

You can predict better for ignorant people than for intelligent people. Intelligent people might do something about it, and that might change everything. The accident-prone person can have cyclical accidents until he finds out that they are cyclic. Then, he knows when they are likely to occur. He becomes more cautious at those times, and usually, he avoids the accident. If everbody in the United States had read the previously quoted predictions about the danger of riots and insurrection, it might have made a difference. Of course, it might not have. Probably, people would not have believed it until *after* it happened. Newspaper, radio and television warnings of the number of people who are going to be killed over a holiday weekend do not seem to cut down the number of killed and injured. Astrology could do better. It could have told in advance which people would be more likely to be killed.

Don't draw any final conclusions about what can and what cannot be done with astrology. With the proper research, much more can be done in the future than can now be done. It will make a great difference if the academic world awakens from its centuries of slumber, in true Rip Van Winkle style, and looks at reality instead of its traditions, textbooks, superstitions and dogma. The medical and psychological worlds would probably have most to gain through astrology, the mother of both subjects. While endorsing astrology for its character analysis accomplishments, both Paracelsus and Eleanor Roosevelt expressed doubts about its capabilities in the realm of prediction, but there was much they did not know about the subject. While the predictions of one astrologer may be wrong, the predictions of another may be consistently correct. It should be noted that both Paracelsus and Dr. Carl Jung endorsed astrology for its accomplishments in diagnosing disease. Dogma and selfishness, as well as brainwashing by the medical schools, have prevented modern medicine from entering this sphere of intelligence. Yet, there are many physicians and some psychologists as well as psychiatrists who are using astrology for diagnosis today, but they are not advertising this fact. Organized medicine would be likely to go on a witch hunt and burn intelligence at the stake.

CHAPTER XI

What about the Psychics?

Astrology is a mathematical phenomenon, nothing more. It is the super mathematical formula being sought by scientists in all of the wrong places. The solar system is a perfectly functioning mathematical unit. Human dynamics function mathematically too, and they function in accord with the same mathematical formula. The more we know about anything, the more we can do about it. Our knowledge of astrology is based on our experience with it, guided by mathematical knowledge that was secretly preserved down through history from the days of unknown civilized antiquity. We are not out of the dark ages, although we are coming along swiftly and more swiftly each year. People with similar horoscopes are similar, and they have similar experiences, and yet, there are differences. The astrologer must bear this in mind. A Mars-Uranus affliction in a chart will make one person lean toward unusual sexual behavior, while it will make another person accident-prone. The astrologer may not be sure which course the dynamic will follow in a particular case, and he must point out that there are several directions in which a force might flow—if forces do flow. However, there is another and far more mysterious phenomenon, and this is the psychic.

The psychic is usually a person born with Neptune or Pisces, or both, very strong in the birth chart. Neptune or Pisces is often on the Ascendent at birth. It is much as if these people were living half in another world. They have a very strange ability. Some of them just appear to be able to look into the future as one would look out a window. This talent is far more common than most folks would suppose. It is estimated that it exists to an observable degree in 20 per cent of the population. It is probably within all of us if we realized it and allowed it to function, but that monster we call society has done everything possible to brainwash it out of us. Dr. J. B. Rhine, formerly of Duke University, has assembled the most data on some phases of the subject. It is more common among savages than among educated people, because our form of education should be classi-fied as brainwashing rather than as education. The writer has had more than 35 years of experience with these people. Duke University accumulated over 10,000 cases of strange psychic experiences. There is nothing new about these people. Ancient literature, including the Bible, has much to say about them, but their abilities are usually called *divine* powers, which means you are not supposed to investigate them. Stay away. They have been called witches. Even to this day, water dowsers are called water witches in the western states.

The psychic is able to suddenly see an event happening in the future, or see an event that is occurring now at great distance. Literature is filled with such cases, but these people have always been persecuted by the churches of our own country. These are the people who were being burned at the stake in Salem and in England by the Christians. They are constantly being ridiculed and called frauds by our fraudulent academicians. They are always persecuted. This persecution has probably been responsible for the rise of the Spritualist Churches. Under the constitution, they can survive if they gather together as a church.

One problem lies in the fact that this psychic ability is not constant. The person having the power cannot call it forth at will. It works without warning, and then it won't work at all. A person has a vision or perhaps a dream in which he sees the future happening before it happens.

This is impossible, according to the accepted and un-proven doctrine of materialism, and this is one of the reasons these people are persecuted and prosecuted so often. If the doctrine of materialism were true, this phenomenon could not happen. The fact that it does happen proves the doctrine of materialism to be wrong. The doctrine is a false teaching. There are greater phe-nomena, greater natural laws than those of physics, but in our monster called society, anything that would upset the doctrine of materialism must be destroyed if pos-sible. It is, nevertheless, difficult to destroy a fact.

Because of their justified fear of persecution, most people having this power do not talk about it. They keep it a secret. Those, who do not, often find them-selves in trouble. The least that can happen to them is that the rank and file will laugh at them and ridicule them. Perhaps the mob will spit on them. Academicians are a part of the mob who most like that spitting proc-ess. The mob can be a beast, and it is a dangerous beast. Intelligent people would not want to be a part of it. Others rush in, hoping to feel its warmth and sweat.

In an effort to gain the approval of materialism, the psychic has practiced many forms of, perhaps justifi-able, deception. Unfortunately, deception is sometimes necessary to survival. One psychic pretends to gain his knowledge from the palm of one's hand, another from numerology, another from astrology. This produces more confusion. What is astrological and what is psychic? The psychic astrologer may actually know little or nothing about astrology, but his predictions may be extremely accurate. The great problem comes when the psychic tries to teach astrology to another. He cannot teach what he does not know. What he teaches may do the student more harm than good. It won't work for the student even if it appears to work for the teacher.

Actually, the true psychic—and this writer has had much experience with good psychics—can do what the astrologer cannot do. He can reach small and sometimes important details that the astrologer can never reach. The astrologer sees what might be compared with the plans of a house. The psychic sees the house and everything in it, including the people. Astrology deals with mathematical designs, not the physical details. A good astrologer must be a good mathematician. Until he knows how mathematics works, he doesn't really know how astrology works.

Remember that the known is the finite, the unknown the infinite. There is much about time that we do not know. If our conception of time, including all scientific conceptions of time, were true, the psychic could not exist. But, psychics have existed all down through history, and they still exist. We find many good ones among the spiritualists, but they fear the so-called scientists, because they have had a taste of their sadistic cruelty. The existence of these people proves that we have some weird misconception of time and space. Nobody has yet come up with even a theory that would explain the psychic in a satisfactory way, but the psychic is a fact, and nothing will ever be honestly scientific so long as facts—any facts at all—have to be excluded. Much of the human mystery we know today exists only because of the universal manner in which facts are excluded by the professionals and the academicians for fear of upsetting that which has become established and which they believe essential to their own personal security. Remember our chapter on Aquarius and Capricorn. Perhaps you should read Chapter IX again. It is important to learn how to distrust authorities, because few authorities are worthy of your trust.

The late Pulitzer prize winning science editor of the *New York Herald Tribune*, John J. O'Neill, spent a great deal of his spare time investigating psychics, astrology and the unknown. He once told the writer, "Even if I find a psychic cheating, I do not accept this as evidence against the existence of psychic ability. Psychics have long been persecuted down through the centuries. They have inferiority complexes. They are insecure, because they do not know at what moment the witch hunters may be knocking at the door. They are often sickly people, because the use of the psychic faculty seems to draw the vital forces out of them when they attempt to force it. There are days when it doesn't function. They do not know why. They are confused by this, and on those days, they may try to fake it. I don't condemn them, because this is important for research. I merely come back another day."

The purpose of this chapter is to make you conscious of the fact that psychism and astrology are two different things. Each subject has its limitations. It is important that you learn to distinguish between the two subjects. Don't mistake one for the other. Keep them separate, but don't under-estimate or over-estimate either. Avoid confusion by not getting the two mixed up. Know with which you are dealing. The astrologer best known during the early part of this century was Evangeline Adams. She was both astrologer and psychic, but her most famous predictions were obviously psychic rather than astrological. This was probably true of Nostradamus and most of the astrologers who lived during the darker ages—those ages that were ever darker than this one.

CHAPTER XII

Karma and Reincarnation

Just as astrology has suffered at the hands of the academic theorists who want to uphold the doctrine of materialism, it has also suffered from the dogmatists intent on upholding the doctrines of karma and reincarnation. There are people who do not believe you can have astrology without accepting karma and reincarnation. Insofar as this writer is concerned, he has never been able to find any evidence for either doctrine. Bear in mind that a lack of evidence does not prove the nonexistence of anything, but it leaves the matter up in the air. Let's look at these two doctrines separately and as they relate to each other.

Karma presents the view that everything good or bad that happens to you in this life is the result of something that you did in a previous life. It is an attempt to make life look just and balanced. However, it isn't very just to be forever punishing people for things they can't remember. It sure doesn't accomplish any objective. You may slap a dog for taking food off the dining room table, and he can get the idea that you don't want him to take food off the dining room table, but if you wait a week until he is out-of-doors, he will not know why you slapped him, and when he returns he will take more food from the table. The reincarnation doctrine is very, very ancient, and it seems to come out of the Orient. Cults have tried to tie it tight to astrology. Karma is like the idea of fate. It implies there is nothing you can do about the situation, but we know differently. When two men are faced with the same problem, one man will face it and solve it, while the other will be too lazy or confused to do anything about it. The result is different. Karma is an excuse for laziness. It causes a man to believe, "There is nothing I can do about it anyhow." It kills ambition. This is one of the things that has held astrology back. This writer was the first person to introduce statistical research into astrology in this country. He was flooded with protests from the old timers in astrology, in effect saying, "You can't do this to us." I was interfering with their lethargy, with their slumbers, with their ignorance. I wasn't informed. They felt they should educate me and let me know that there is nothing we can do about it. BUNK!

This writer's own experience since 1926, when he first became interested in astrology, disproves to his satisfaction the whole theme of karma. Don't you turn against it just because of this writer's experience. Think it out for yourself. On the other hand, don't accept karma as a doctrine until you see some evidence of its truth. Up till now, it can be considered nothing more than a dogma, with no evidence to back it up. More than that, it appears to be a very harmful doctrine. It has held back the civilizations which believed it. In our own time, the astrologers who believed the doctrine have done nothing for astrology. They have held back its progress. Some of the prejudice against astrology has come from those who merely familiarized themselves with these theories without investigating astrology itself. Because karma didn't fit with known facts, they assumed that astrology didn't either. Thus, if you are interested in going on to study astrology, it would be this writer's advice to skip karma until someone can produce some evidence for it. There has been no evidence produced up till now, and that makes it just as dangerous as the doctrine of materialism. Certain religions have indoctrinated people into the belief in karma. When karma is accepted, all progress seems to stop. It held back the Orient for centuries.

Reincarnation is the doctrine which tells us that before we were born here we lived in another body at a different time, and that when we leave here we will be re-born into another body. Each such life is considered an incarnation. Some people claim to remember past lives. Do you remember any? This writer has never been able to find any evidence for or against the doctrine, and before accepting it, we should have some evidence to consider. We have none.

How can we tell whether a person who claims to remember past lives is actually remembering past lives or is remembering something akin to dreams? A dream can be very vivid, so vivid at times that upon awakening, an individual may not be sure whether it was a dream or whether it actually happened. We have other cases, where a person in a trance or in a state of hypnosis appears to remember previous lives, as in the Bridey Murphy case, but here again, how do we know this is not all imagination. It might be similar to a dream. The person in a state of hypnosis is inclined to want to please the person asking questions, and if the hypnotist is asking questions about past lives, the person under hypnosis might be able to imagine some up just to please the hypnotist. There are people who can do this without being in a trance, while they are wide awake. We are merely reasoning. We are not gaining any fact, but our purpose is to avoid *beliefs* when we have no evidence, because beliefs become mental blocks and prevent us from bothering to look for evidence either pro or con. If we believe something, then we look only for evidence which would appear to confirm the belief. A true scientist should have no beliefs. He should never stop looking for new evidence.

If the consciousness, or the soul, as the theologist would call it, exists now, how could it not have always existed, or how can it ever cease to exist? Matter can exist in different forms, but it still exists. Ice can change into fluid water. An abstraction has permanent existence —the Pythagorean theorem for example. It has always existed, even if people were not conscious of it. It exists now, and it always will exist. Only the form of something can change. You can build a house out of blocks, knock it down and build another kind of a house out of the same blocks. The blocks continue to exist, but the form of the house changes. If the consciousness or soul exists now, it must have a permanence, and it must have always existed, although its form may have changed. By this reasoning, and this is only reasoning and might be wrong, the consciousness or soul must always exist. Thus, while we have no evidence that reincarnation is true, neither do we have any evidence that it is not true. So let us keep an open mind until we can find some evidence one way or the other.

There is something else to think about. If souls are

reincarnating on this earth, where are all the new ones coming from? The population has been constantly increasing throughout known history. All these new people couldn't be the same ones who were here before in past lives. There are too many of them. It doesn't add up.

There is another doctrine called the transmigration of souls. You might have been an animal in a past life. If an animal, why not an insect? There are many insects. The mosquito population alone is much greater than the human population. If you are one of those new souls, perhaps you were an insect in past life. If you were human, perhaps you came from another planet or another universe.

Let's face it. We don't know, and when we don't know, let's say so. Let's refrain from fooling ourselves, and why try to fool others. Self-deception is the worst kind. Others cannot deceive you unless you are willing to fool yourself. Any person who accepts an unproved doctrine or scientific theory without legitimate proof is fooling himself. If you are going to study astrology, start out right. Don't accept any doctrines. Investigate. Look for facts, and keep testing. If a rule works 99 out of 100 times, never mind the 99 times. Find out *WHY* it didn't happen the other time. You won't have any trouble remembering the 99 cases that worked, but don't toss out that one case that didn't work. Keep it for further investigation.

The writer often receives letters saying, "How can you accept astrology and not accept karma and reincarnation?" In other words, everything has to be a package deal. This too is the result of brain-washing. Most people do not like to have to think for themselves. They would prefer to merely repeat what they have heard. They seek a savior who knows all. They'll never have to think again. A textbook often serves the same purpose as the savior. Mental lethargy is desirable to a great many people.

Instead of looking for a package deal, instead of accepting astrology as a package, why not accept only that which works for you. In that way, you will not be deceiving yourself. The astrologers who have accepted karma and reincarnation as a part of astrology have made no progress. They are very confused beings. Let's stick to what we can prove while we keep on looking and investigating to see what else may be either true or false. This is the only true scientific attitude, although a lot of so-called scientists do not have it.

Even karma and reincarnation should not be accepted or rejected as a package. There are greater possibilities of reincarnation being true than of karma being true. Most ancient civilizations within our knowledge believed in reincarnation. Christ appears to have believed in reincarnation, although the Christian Church does not. Those of us who work with astrology know there is something we can do about any given situation. It depends upon how much understanding we have. The more we understand, the more we can handle. After we understood the laws of planetary motion and those of gravity, which are mathematical laws, we were able to put up satellites. Finally, we were able to send up probes and take pictures of the Moon and radio them back to earth. Then, we were able to send cameras 135,000,000 miles and take pictures of the planet Mars, but first, there was much that we had to understand. The purpose in drawing up a horoscope is to understand the person who was born at that time. If you understand the person, you can help him. Dr. Carl Jung found that if he could see the horoscope of a patient, his understanding obtained thereform would enable him to help the patient. If you believed in karma, then you wouldn't do any of this, because you would believe that cause was working itself out, and that there would be nothing anybody could do about it. It would be like fate, but what about the men who don't believe in karma and who go forth and build new empires? Where would our space program be if the space scientists believed that there is nothing they can do about our current status? Most of the real problems that individuals and civilization as a whole have are due to false beliefs. Give this serious thought before you allow yourself to accept *any beliefs*. Don't believe in astrology. Merely investigate it and learn what you can do with it to help yourself and others. The first thing it will do is to give you greater understanding.

CHAPTER XIII

Time and Space

There is something about our conceptions of time and space that does not add up. According to scientific conceptions, light travels at 186,000 miles per second. That means that it takes something over a second for light to travel from the Moon to the earth, so that when you look at the Moon, you are seeing it as it was a second previously. You are not seeing it as it is at this exact moment. In that time, the Moon moved about 17 miles. The Sun is farther away. You see it as it was about 8 minutes before. You look out at the stars. They are very far away, but all at different distances. One star will be 100 light years away. You are looking at it as it was before you were born, 100 years ago. Another star is a million light years away. You are looking a million years into the past. You don't even know whether the star is still there. It may have been destroyed at some time during the last million years. Think about this, and you will realize that since the only thing you ever see is light, with your eyes, you can see only in one direction. Physical sight looks only into the past.

Yet, the psychic looks in the opposite direction. He looks within himself, and he sees into the future. How about that? The psychic may turn his physical sight to a crystal ball. This merely takes his own inner attention away from the outer world, enabling him to better see into his inner world. Some psychics use a teacup full of grounds. There is nothing in the crystal. There is nothing but grounds in the tea cup. However, these concentrate physical sight to a point of monotony where nothing is moving, and allows the inner sight to take over. The psychic then appears to see into the future. There are days when he cannot see much of anything in this inner world. There are also days when he cannot see much in the outer world either. He cannot see eight minutes into the past, because clouds have completely blotted out the Sun. Thus, this inner sight into the future is as faulty as our physical sight into the past.

Now, let's look at another strange set of facts.

Astrologers associate a planet or solar object with each sign of the zodiac. Yet, to complete a design, there would have to be two more planets beyond Pluto. Let us note this association:

Cancer	Moon
Leo	Sun
Virgo	Mercury
Libra	Venus
Scorpio	Mars
Sagittarius	Jupiter
Capricorn	Saturn
Aquarius	Uranus
Pisces	Neptune
Aries	Pluto
Taurus	"Y"
Gemini	"Z"

In the left-hand column, we have the zodiacal signs exactly as we find them around the circle, beginning with the summer solstice. In the right-hand column, we have the planets and solar objects in the exact order of their mean distance from the earth. The Moon is nearest, the Sun next, etc. This is a striking coincidence, if it is a coincidence. The writer first noticed this sequence in September of 1933. Until that time, nobody had ever noted that the sequences corresponded. The ancients had started this sequence, employing only seven bodies. When Uranus was discovered, it was ultimately associated with Aquarius, not because of the sequence, but because the astrologers found similar associations relative to human characteristics. Yet, unconsciously, they followed the sequence. The same thing happened when

Neptune was discovered and it was associated with Pisces. When Pluto was discovered, some of the astrologers associated it with Aries, which continued the sequence, while others, studying Greek mythology, came up with the idea that it should be associated with Scorpio. The ancients said that Jupiter rules Sagittarius, which could mean Jupiter measures Sagittarius, which can mean that when you count out six bodies, beginning with the Moon, you come to Jupiter, and when you count six signs beginning with Cancer, you come to Sagittarius.

Going out to the dividing line between Saturn and Uranus, it is odd that we find Saturn associated with the past, Uranus associated with the future. Going around the circle from Cancer, we find Capricorn associated with the past, Aquarius associated with the future. The writer finds that this can be extended. Every other sign appears to be associated with consciousness of the past, while the remaining odd signs are associated with consciousness of the future. All of this is completely foreign to anything known by the world of science. It is even foreign to anything known by psychologists, who are supposed to be concerned with the human mind.

There is a tendency to deny anything we cannot explain—or to ignore it and go on our way. So-called science cannot explain astrology, and it cannot explain psychic phenomena. So, first it denies it. If that doesn't work, it ignores it. "That's something we don't talk about." When small children ask where babies come from, some parents do not want to explain it because of their own guilt complexes, and so, they say, "That's something we don't talk about."

The past no longer exists, and yet we can see it when we look at a star 100 million light years away. When we look through a telescope, we can see farther and farther back into the past.

Scientists talk about an expanding universe. But, they are looking out farther and farther away and farther and farther into the past. It becomes impossible to see all the objects as they are now. We don't see any of them as they are now. We see each one as it was at a different time. Thus, what we think we see is quite something else from what is there now. Suppose we were to look into a room and see one man who was there on Monday, a second man who was there on Tuesday, and a third man who was there on Wednesday. It would appear that the men had been together, and yet, they were not.

Considering all of these strange facts, we are forced to ask whether our common conception of time and space might possibly be far different from the truth. We can only ask the question. We cannot answer it. We do suggest keeping an open mind about time and space because if we do, we are always able to consider new evidence that might turn up tomorrow. If we close our minds, we will be unlikely to see the evidence if it appears. Astrologers find that the geometric movement of the planets will tell us a certain amount about future trends. We know of no reason why this should be so. We know only that it is so. On the other hand, scientists, particularly biologists, know that plants, animals and people grow. They do not know why they grow—nor how. There is no known fact that is more mysterious than growth, and yet, science cannot explain it. Geologists know that minerals form, and in accord with geometrical designs. They do not know how nor why. Nobody denies either growth nor crystalization because they are so common and so many people know about them. Aside from foreigners in that country, no scientist in India would deny astrology, because too many people know about it.

Some Oriental beliefs claim that the past, present and future are coexistent. As we know time and space, we cannot visualize that possibility. It would be something like a man traveling from New York to Chicago. When he has reached the half-way mark, he cannot see either New York nor Chicago, but they are there. They do exist. New York and Chicago are coexistent.

When the astrologer predicts the future, he is merely calculating. Because of what is known about the mathematics of the solar system, it is possible to predict where it has been at any given time in the past. The astrologer knows from experience that when Uranus crosses the birth position of a person's Sun, a series of great changes occurs in his life. Because he can compute when Uranus will be there, he can also compute and predict when those great changes will take place. Could the mystery of the psychic be explained in some similar fashion.

Some modern saviors believe that ultimate electronic computers will be superior to man. What these saviors overlook is the fact that while men can make computers, computers cannot make men. The computer is merely a slave of man. It can accomplish only what man has determined and designed it to do.

If it is allowed to function, the human mind includes a computer far superior to any electronic device ever built. It can design electronic computers. It can do what computers cannot do. It can explore the unknown and come up with new mathematical formulas, which it can teach a computer to apply.

There is just as much to investigate within one human mind as there is to investigate out in space, even if you go all the way to infinity. Men like Sir Isaac Newton are able to find out what is going on out in space merely by retiring into their own minds. They determine how to predict the exact moment of tomorrow's sunrise, and in doing so, they are seeing into the future.

Down through history, there have been child prodigies, small children with some mysterious ability to out-compute the most educated mathematicians. The academicians have called these children *savant idiots*. They are considered idiots because they are not like other children. A vast number of academicians want everybody to be exactly alike. That's why they often have people wear uniforms. If they are not alike, the academicians intend making them alike. We have laws determining that everybody—all children—must go to one of our schools, where it can be brainwashed and made like all the other children. Without exception, the child prodigy is forced into one of these brainwashing institutions, where his special talents are brainwashed out of him. In time, his mentality is dulled and society has been served. The monster has devoured another victim.

How do these pieces fit together?

There are a great many people whose minds have done extraordinary calculating while the individual was asleep, making it possible to awaken with the answer to a problem the individual had been unable to solve while awake. This phenomenon has occurred to this writer many times. It has occurred with many other people. It is not too unusual. Therefore, consider the possibilities open to the abstract computer system which is all a part of the mind of each and every one of us and which we could use if we knew how.

With the knowledge we now have at hand, it would be quite easy to construct an electronic astrologer which could do as much predicting as astrologers in human form now do. Just lend us Westinghouse or IBM for a little while, and we could easily produce such a being, because the astrologer merely records data and employs mathematical laws in computing the future. He doesn't yet have to think up any new laws, because he can employ the same ones that function in connection with the solar system.

Consider how dead and unconscious we were insofar as a space program was concerned before the Russians put up a satellite. Remember how our great leader in the Whitehouse, President Dwight Eisenhower, ridiculed the idea, saying he wasn't interested in making a little ball fly around the earth. Only under public pressure was he willing to do anything about it, or permit others to do anything about it. An astronomer in England gave a statement to the press, in which he described the proposed space program as nonsense, and said it would be much better to spend the money to buy him a new telescope. We would still be looking at Mars from the earth.

If the ability of the psychic is actually the work of a complex computer system that exists within his own mind (not his brain), then we would find it less mysterious, and we could continue to hang on to our present concepts of time and space. If it is not, then we are in trouble, because it will be necessary to seek some far more complex explanation which might completely undermine our whole scientific concept of time and space.

This book has been a very preliminary discussion of astrology. You can go very deep. You can go as deep as you may be prepared to go. You can go into it a mile or a million miles. Which do you want it to be? There is no limit. You can go into it a little bit and enjoy yourself, or you can take it more seriously, and perhaps you can solve a problem that no other person has ever been able to solve.

Whatever we have done in space up till now could have been accomplished many years before. It wasn't, because so large a ratio of people do not want to do anything different from the manner in which it was done yesterday. There is no richer field for research in the world today than astrology offers. Society has not awakened to its actual possibilities. It is still satisfied to use astrology as a source of entertainment. Even the code of the national broadcasters states that it can be placed on radio and television only as a matter of entertainment, unless you want to say something against it. This clause was instigated by the professional jealousy of the academic astronomers, who want everybody to think alike—the way they think or dream.

After the insurrection of Los Angeles, with its millions of dollars in damage, its fires, its deaths and its injuries, a U.S. Senator from California went on television and stated that this was something that no one could predict. Yet, it was predicted in *BORDERLINE* Magazine, where it was stated that blood could run in the streets. Practically all astrological publications repeatedly warned President John Kennedy of the danger of assassination. This writer talked about it in print in the *Tucson Daily Citizen* as far back as 1958. The great fire of London had been predicted by the astrologer John Lilly. He was called before a parlimentary investigation. How could he have predicted the fire if he didn't start it. The writer would be in a mess if he were accused of having caused all the things he predicted in advance, such as the Negro riots and insurrections of 1964 and 1965, the assassination of President Kennedy, the death in office of President Franklin D. Roosevelt, the Russian overthrow of Beria in July of 1953 and hundreds of minor events. The late astrologer Alma Granning would have been in trouble for predicting to the month the death of Stalin. John Hazelrigg would have been in trouble for predicting the death while in office of President Warren G. Harding, while another astrologer would have had to face the fact that he predicted the assassination of Abraham Lincoln.

Society has its choice. It can confine interest in astrology to entertainment or it can investigate its possibilities of bringing a new understanding of life to civilization.